SOCKS
FROM THE TOE UP

ESSENTIAL TECHNIQUES AND PATTERNS FROM WENDY KNITS

WENDY D. JOHNSON

POTTER
CRAFT
NEW YORK

TENTS

INTRODUCTION

Once upon a time, I was just a girl who wanted to knit socks. I started knitting socks after I was seduced by the self-striping yarns that first appeared a few years back. Anything that appears to work by magic amuses and entertains me, so I was hooked after my first peek at some sock yarn that knit up into tiger stripes.

I decided then that I wanted to knit my socks from the toe up. The most compelling reason for this is that I have always loathed grafting. Another reason is that it's ideal when you have a limited quantity of yarn. With a toe-up pattern I can knit until I run out of yarn, thus eliminating any anxiety about having enough to finish the sock.

I commute to my office by train, and sock knitting seemed like the perfect way to occupy my travel time. I wanted to make the process as simple and easy as possible, so I did some research on knitting socks toe-up and settled on the techniques that seemed the simplest: a provisional cast-on, a short-row toe, and a short-row heel. I worked up a pattern incorporating these techniques and memorized this pattern.

I later refined and wrote up a generic pattern for toe-up socks that could be used as a formula for any sock at any gauge and posted it on my website. Hundreds, if not thousands, of knitters have used that pattern, altering it to suit their gauge and foot size.

I fell out of love with socks for a year or two, until a friend requested a pair of hand-knit socks. I whipped out my generic pattern, knit the socks, and once again found myself hooked. I happily knit socks using my formula for another year.

A couple of years ago, all that changed. I became bored with my short rows and started experimenting with other toe and heel techniques. I worked up a couple more generic patterns with two different gusseted heels that mimicked the look of top-down socks but that were knit toe-up. And I started knitting all my socks using those generic patterns.

Shortly thereafter, I heard about a project that was forming in the online knitting world: the Summer of Socks 2007. The idea was to spend the summer focused on knitting socks. Whether to knit socks exclusively or mix them in with other projects was up to each individual participant. There would be contests and games and other assorted high jinks. Because it sounded like fun and there were very few rules, I decided to join in.

"Hey! Just for fun, let's see how many socks I can design myself and knit up during the Summer of Socks," I thought to myself. I got out the graph paper and pencils and got to work.

At the end of the summer, I had nineteen pairs of socks completed. Out of those nineteen pairs of socks, eighteen were my own original designs.

But I was not done with sock design. I kept writing toe-up sock patterns and knitting them. And that is how this book came into being.

The patterns I've included range from easy to challenging and include lace, cables, and texture. I've also included plain basic sock patterns with the three different heels that I like best, which you can use as a starting point to create your own original sock designs. In designing the projects for this book, my goal was to create patterns that are fun to knit and pleasing to the eye while still being comfortable to wear. I hope you enjoy knitting them as much as I enjoyed creating them.

PART 1: TOE-UP ESSENTIALS

TOOLS FOR SOCK KNITTING

SO YOU WANT TO KNIT SOCKS? TO START OFF ON THE RIGHT FOOT, YOU NEED THE RIGHT STUFF. YOU WON'T NEED MANY TOOLS IN ORDER TO KNIT SOCKS AND THEY NEED NOT BE EXPENSIVE, BUT YOU WILL WANT TO CHOOSE CAREFULLY TO AVOID FRUSTRATION DOWN THE LINE.

NEEDLE CHOICES

The most important and the only really necessary tool for sock knitters? No surprise there: knitting needles!

Knitting needles are available in a variety of materials, including bamboo, wood, metal, and plastic. Which material you choose is part personal preference and part practicality. Are you a new knitter or new to knitting socks? Try using wooden needles, as they have a bit of "grab" to them and will cling to your stitches. If you are using a particularly slippery yarn, such as some silk blends, a wooden needle will be less likely to slip out of your stitches as you work. As you gain experience and want to speed up your knitting, you can switch to faster, metal needles, which, because of their smooth surface, allow stitches to slide off the tips quickly and smoothly. If you are using a yarn with some texture, such as some cotton/lycra blends, you might want to use metal instead of wood needles because the yarn won't cling to the smooth surface of the metal needles. If you have a tendency to snap wooden needles, try using metal needles. You'll be hard-pressed to break those. Do metal needles seem too cold? Try needles that warm up with your body heat, such as wood or plastic. There's no rule that says you have to use the same needles for every sock you knit; knit with the needles that work best for the yarn you are using.

There are three ways to knit socks in the round: on double-pointed needles, on two circular needles, or on one circular needle employing what is called the Magic Loop technique. These different needle methods are described in detail in the techniques section on page 12.

DOUBLE-POINTED NEEDLES

Double-pointed needles used to come in sets of four in the United States but, happily, have popped up in sets of five in recent years. Double-pointed needles have typically come in sets of five in other parts of the world, so perhaps we have the Internet and easier global communication to thank for making them popular in the United States as well. I think a set of five works better than a set of four. Using a set of five double-pointed needles, you have your stitches divided over four needles and use the fifth needle to knit. Not only does this make it easier to differentiate the sole stitches from the instep stitches, but having your stitches divided over four needles rather than three reduces the chance of "ladders," or loose stitches at the junction of the needles, because less strain is put on the stitches at the joins. Double-pointed needles are available in a variety of lengths, from 4" to 10" (10cm–25.5cm) long, with lots of length choices in between. I happen to own several sets of 14"- (35.5cm-) long steel double-pointed needles in very small needle sizes that look particularly dangerous. I wouldn't recommend using these to knit socks, unless you want your needles to double as weapons—you could easily injure anyone who gets too close to you while you are knitting!

I find 6" (15cm) double-pointed needles to be easiest to use for knitting socks. Any smaller and the ends of the needles have a tendency to poke me in the palms of my hands. Any larger and I'm slowed down and annoyed by the need to slide my work from end to end of the needles.

TWO CIRCULAR NEEDLES

Knitting socks on two circular needles has become my favorite method. You need two circular needles of the same size (for example, 2mm needles) but not necessarily of the same cable length. Some knitters like to use two needles with differing cable lengths because they can tell at a glance which needle is which. Some people prefer shorter circular needles, 16" (40.5cm), for example, while others are more comfortable with needles that are at least 24" (61cm) long. It really is a matter of personal preference, what you find most comfortable, and what length of needles you happen to have on hand.

ONE LONG CIRCULAR NEEDLE

One sock-knitting technique enables you to knit with one long circular needle. To execute this technique, start with a needle that is at least 40" (101.5cm) long—48" (122cm) is even better. Some people prefer a shorter needle, but it's easier to learn the technique with a longer one. Because you will be manipulating the needle cable, choose a needle that has a nice flexible cable and a smooth join.

OTHER TOOLS

Although needles should be your number one concern, there are other tools you can use to make your sock knitting life easier.

STITCH MARKERS

You generally will not need a stitch marker to mark the beginning of the round when knitting socks, because the beginning of the round will be at a junction between needles. Stitch markers can be useful nevertheless. If your sock pattern has pattern "repeats" or is complicated, use stitch markers to set out each design element of the pattern. In a pinch, use circles cut from a plastic drinking straw or tie yarn of a contrasting color into a loop on your needle.

ROW COUNTER

Although it is not always necessary to count the rows in your sock knitting, you may find it easier to keep track of where you are by doing so. Also, by counting rows, you can ensure that two socks in a pair will match exactly.

If you are knitting a pattern that contains a repeat of a certain number of rows, you may also find a row counter helpful. Use a handheld "kacha-kacha"-style row counter. The barrel-style counter that you slip onto a needle is convenient because it stays with your work, but it won't work very well for sock knitting in the round because you need to keep moving it to make any progress.

TIP If you have only a barrel-style row counter, pin it to your knitting with an oversized safety pin.

TAPE MEASURE OR RULER

If you are not counting rows with a row counter, you'll need some sort of measuring device, such as a tape measure or a ruler. If you're carrying your knitting with you as you travel, you might want to tuck a tape measure in your bag as part of your standard traveling equipment. I can't tell you how many times I have found myself without a measuring device when I really needed one. At one point, I considered having my arm tattooed with a ruler, in both inches and centimeters, but sanity prevailed in the end. I finally wised up and now keep an inexpensive tape measure or short ruler in all my tote bags and purses.

TIP: A standard U.S. business card measures exactly $3\frac{1}{2}$" by 2" (9cm × 5cm) and makes a great portable measuring device. I mark a business card in half-inch (13mm) increments to make it even more useful. Of course, every time I forget and give that card to a business contact, I have to make another mini ruler!

COILLESS SAFETY PINS

I also use coilless pins as a measuring device. I knit socks on my commute, and I am constantly switching purses and knitting bags. Despite my good intentions to keep one in every bag I own, my tape measure is sometimes left behind. Before leaving the house or the office, I measure my work and place a coilless pin to mark a specific measurement. For example, when I am making socks for myself, I usually knit to 7 inches (18cm) or so before starting the increase for the gusset. If I'm ready to leave for work and I've got slightly more than 5" (12.5cm) done, I'll place a pin at the 5" mark. Because I know my row gauge, I can count the rows from 5" and know when I've reached 7" (18cm). You can also place a pin at the start of gusset increases to make it easier to count the number of increases as you complete them. Coilless pins also make great stitch markers and mini stitch holders.

CABLE NEEDLE

If you are doing a cabled sock and you aren't a "cable without a cable needle" kind of knitter, this is an important tool. A toothpick might work in a pinch, but surprisingly, I do not often find myself in the presence of toothpicks.

TAPESTRY NEEDLES

One of the joys of toe-up socks is that they require no grafting. Still, you are going to have at least two ends to weave in, one at the beginning of the sock and one at the end. And if you want to work the tubular bind-off, you will need a tapestry needle to graft your stitches at the end.

SCISSORS

You will, after all, have to cut your yarn when you've finished your sock. (I have been known to gnaw through a strand of yarn when I didn't have scissors handy, but I don't recommend it, nor am I proud of it. It also draws strange looks from my fellow commuters.)

A NOTEBOOK AND/OR STICKY NOTES

A small notebook to keep track of your sock knitting can be one of your most valuable tools. I often make notations about the sock I am knitting on a sticky note affixed to the pattern, so that I have the information handy when I start the second sock.

SOCK BLOCKERS

These can be used to shape your socks after washing. To block or not to block? That is the question. Truthfully, when I wash my socks, I do not block them because I figure that they block out nicely on the actual foot. But if you keep a photographic record of your sock knitting like I do, sock blockers are a great way to display your sock masterpieces.

YARNS FOR SOCK KNITTING

ONE OF MY MOTTOS IS "SOCK YARN DOES NOT COUNT AS STASH," AND I WILL DEFEND THAT IN THE FACE OF ALL OPINIONS TO THE CONTRARY.

Sock yarn is my favorite indulgence. It is an affordable one because you need only buy one or two skeins of yarn to make a pair of socks. When I look at my skeins of sock yarns, I think of them as little jewels, small luxuries that glow with colors that make me happy. I decorate with sock yarn, putting skeins in baskets and bowls in my living room.

Just a few years ago, there were only a few sock yarns available for sale: solid colors in sturdy wool/nylon blends that were rugged and practical. Then the self-striping sock yarns came on the scene. Recently, hand-painted sock yarns by "indie dyers" have started popping up in small online shops. Now, sock yarns are available in a rainbow of colors and a variety of different fibers.

What do you look for in a sock yarn? For starters, most of the time you want to use a yarn that's easy to care for. Superwash wool is a good choice, so you can machine-wash your socks. A lot of people do hand-wash their superwash wool socks to make them last longer, but I throw mine in the washer on the gentle cycle. I will put them in the dryer, too, if I am in a hurry, but I try to take them out while they are still slightly damp. If you want your socks to last as long as possible, a blend with some nylon in it is a good idea. You want a yarn that's very soft, like merino wool. A yarn with a tight twist will, of course, be more durable than one that is loosely spun.

Sock yarns are available in many different fibers and blends: wool, alpaca, cashmere, silk, bamboo, cot-ton, and so on. If you live in a warm climate, cotton is a good choice for your hand-knit socks, but look for a cotton yarn with a bit of something stretchy, like Lycra, blended into it, so the socks will keep their shape and not sag and bag on you.

The truth is that many nonsock yarns can be pressed into service for socks. With these, you will generally want to knit at a tighter gauge than recommended on the yarn's ball band. For example, I usually knit DK and worsted-weight yarns at a sportweight gauge (6 stitches to 1" [2.5cm]) for socks, instead of the stated gauge of 5 stitches or fewer to the inch. Knitting very firmly makes a stronger, tighter fabric that will resist wear.

A word of caution about hand-painted and hand-dyed sock yarns: the more intricate your sock pattern, the less variegated you want your sock yarn to be. There's nothing more disheartening than meticulously knitting a complex lace pattern and having it obscured by a too-wildly-variegated yarn. There are many beautiful sock yarns available in solid colors, almost-solid colors, and subtle heathers. While a lot of the patterns in this book will look best in these non-variegated yarns, a few will look great in your wildest hand-paints, as noted in the descriptions for those patterns.

You can have a lot of fun using different yarns in your sock knitting. You can have just as much fun collecting skeins of sock yarn. Remember, sock yarn does not count as stash!

HOW TO SPLIT A SKEIN OF SOCK YARN INTO TWO EVEN BALLS

One advantage of knitting socks from the toe up is that you can knit until you run out of yarn. But what do you do if your sock yarn comes in one skein large enough to knit a pair of socks? Easy—you split the skein in half. To do this, you'll need some sort of apparatus for winding your skein into a ball (either a swift and ball winder or your own two hands) and a scale. (I use an inexpensive digital kitchen scale set to weigh in grams, and it works great.)

Wind your skein into a ball, and weigh the ball on the scale. Make a note of the weight and divide it by two.

Start winding a second ball from the first ball. From time to time, weigh the original ball. When the original ball is half of its former weight, cut the yarn so that you now have two balls of about equal weight. If your sock yarn is self-striping, you might want to rewind the half that was the original ball of yarn so that both balls are now wound in the same direction; otherwise your striping sequence will be reversed.

SOCK-KNITTING TECHNIQUES

HOW DO YOU KNIT A TOE-UP SOCK? AS YOU MIGHT EXPECT, YOU START AT THE TOE, WORK YOUR WAY UP THE FOOT, WORK A HEEL, AND THEN THE LEG. BUT FIRST, YOU NEED TO TAKE SOME KEY MEASUREMENTS OF THE RECIPIENT'S FOOT TO ENSURE THAT THE SOCK WILL FIT NICELY.

MEASURING THE FOOT

First, you want to measure the circumference of the foot at its widest point, which is usually around the ball of the foot. Subtract 10 percent from this measurement because you'll want a bit of negative ease for the sock to fit properly. The resulting number is the measurement you will use for the circumference of the sock.

The next measurement you need is the length of the foot from the tip of the longest toe to the point where the ankle starts to join the foot.

It also helps to measure around the leg just above the ankle. If the circumference of the leg (minus the 10 percent, like the foot measurement) differs vastly from the foot circumference measurement, make a note of that and adjust the number of stitches accordingly (up or down) after you turn the heel and start knitting the leg of the sock. If you are knitting a patterned sock that requires an exact number of stitches to make the pattern come put properly, you can make this measurement adjustment by going up or down a needle size.

A WORD ABOUT GAUGE

Gauge in sock knitting is vitally important. One stitch off in gauge, and you will have either a sock that is too loose and keeps falling down the leg and sagging on the foot or one that is too tight and that will not slip on easily over the heel and ankle. For example, if your sock is 64 stitches around and the stated gauge is 8 stitches to 1" (2.5cm), you will end up with a sock that is 8" (20.5cm) in circumference. If your gauge is off and you knit at 7 stitches to the inch, your sock will end up being 9" (23cm) around, and if you knit at 9 stitches to the inch, the sock will end up being 7" (18cm) around. As you can see, one stitch makes a big difference in gauge. Whereas some stitch patterns are very stretchy and can accommodate variances in gauge, others (such as some cabled patterns) are not and must be knit to gauge for best result.

I highly recommend knitting a gauge swatch if you are using a sock yarn for the first time. If your gauge for knitting in the round varies from your gauge for knitting flat, as it does for many people, you will need to knit your gauge swatch in the

round. Cast on enough stitches for a tube with a circumference of at least 4" (10cm) (though more is better!), join, and knit for several inches before measuring.

After you have determined your gauge, you can easily find your "magic number"—the number of stitches you need for a sock to fit properly. For example, if the foot you are knitting for is 9" (23cm) around, subtract 10 percent from that and you get $8\frac{1}{10}$" (you can round down to 8" [20.5cm]). So if your sock gauge is 8 stitches per inch, a sock knitted with 64 stitches will fit that foot nicely.

OK, now suppose you have a sock pattern that is knit over 64 stitches and your magic number for a perfect fit is 60 stitches. If the pattern allows it, you can remove a couple of stitches here and there. But if it's a patterned sock that won't work on 60 stitches, you can fudge a little by tightening up your gauge, either by going down a needle size or by consciously knitting a little bit tighter than usual.

Note that there is a suggested needle size for all the patterns in this book. This is a starting point for your gauge swatch. Every knitter is different, so you will not necessarily get the stated gauge with the needle size suggested. You may already know that you usually get the gauge stated in these patterns with a different needle size, so that is the size you'll want to use when you start swatching. If you don't already know it, knit some swatches on different sizes of needles until you get the appropriate gauge.

TECHNIQUES FOR CREATING TOES

AS I MENTIONED EARLIER, ALL TOE-UP SOCKS START, NOT SURPRISINGLY, WITH A TOE. THERE ARE A NUMBER OF DIFFERENT TECHNIQUES FOR CASTING ON AND KNITTING THE TOE OF A TOE-UP SOCK. MY FAVORITES ARE DEMONSTRATED HERE. ALL OF THESE CAST-ON TECHNIQUES ARE DEMONSTRATED OVER TWO CIRCULAR NEEDLES BUT COULD JUST AS EASILY BE EXECUTED USING ONE LONG CIRCULAR IN THE MAGIC LOOP TECHNIQUE. WITH THE EXCEPTION OF THE SHORT-ROW TOE, I RECOMMEND USING EITHER TWO CIRCULAR NEEDLES OR ONE LONG CIRCULAR FOR YOUR CAST-ON INSTEAD OF DOUBLE-POINTED NEEDLES, BECAUSE WITH EACH YOU ARE CREATING TWO SETS OF STITCHES PARALLEL TO EACH OTHER. WITH A CIRCULAR NEEDLE, YOU CAN MOVE THE SET OF STITCHES NOT BEING WORKED TO THE CABLE OF THE NEEDLE, MAKING IT MUCH EASIER TO KNIT THE STITCHES THAT ARE IN PLAY.

SHORT-ROW TOE

This demonstration is based on a sock that is 48 stitches around. It is started by provisionally casting on half of the total sock stitches, in this case, 24.

Using scrap yarn in a color different from the sock yarn being used, crochet a chain that is several chain stitches longer than the number of knit stitches you need. Use a smooth nonfuzzy yarn for the chain—picking up stitches in a chain crocheted from mohair or bouclé is not easy! For a 24-stitch cast-on, I usually make my chain about 30 stitches long. Bind off the last stitch and cut the yarn. Tie a knot in this tail of yarn; you are going to "unzip" this provisional cast-on later by undoing and pulling on this end, so the knot will make the right end easier to find.

Look at the chain. One side of it will be smooth and look like a row of little Vs. The other side will have a bump in the center of each V.

Using your sock yarn and two double-pointed needles (or one circular needle), knit 1 stitch into the bump in the center of each little V on the back side of the chain until you have 24 stitches (see Short Row Toe 1).

Purl back across the stitches. You are ready to start the short rows.

Row 1 Knit 23 stitches. With the yarn in front, slip the last stitch from the left needle to the right needle (see Short Row Toe 2). Turn your work.

Row 2 Slip the first, unworked stitch from the left needle onto the right needle. Purl the next stitch (you will have wrapped that first stitch around its base with the working yarn), and purl across the next 21 stitches in the row. Move the working yarn as if to knit and slip the last stitch. Turn.

Row 3 Slip the first stitch and knit across to the last stitch before the unworked stitch. Wrap and turn.

Row 4 Slip the first stitch and purl across to the stitch before the unworked stitch. Wrap and turn. Continue working rows 3 and 4 in this manner (see Short Row Toe 3).

Work until 8 of the toe stitches are wrapped and on the left side, 8 stitches are "live" in the middle, and 8 are wrapped and on the right. At this stage, you should be ready to work a right-side row. Your toe is half done.

Note: The number of stitches you leave unworked in the middle depends on how wide you want your sock toe to be. If you want it a bit wider, do a couple fewer short rows. If you want it a bit narrower, do a couple more short rows.

NOW WORK THE SECOND HALF OF THE TOE:

Row 1 Knit across the live stitches to the first unworked, wrapped stitch. On the next stitch, pick up the wrap and knit it together with the wrapped stitch.

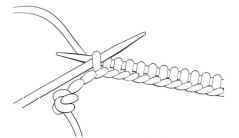

Short Row Toe 1

Note: The wrap sits almost horizontal around the vertical stitch. Put your needle through the horizontal wrap, then the vertical stitch, and then knit the two together (see Short Row Toe 4).

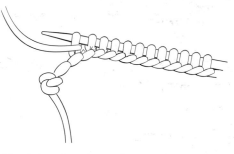

Short Row Toe 2

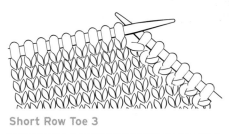

Short Row Toe 3

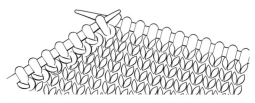

Short Row Toe 4

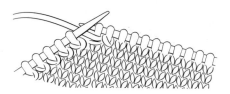

Short Row Toe 5

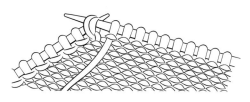

Short Row Toe 6

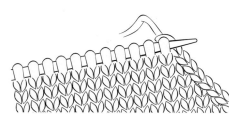

Short Row Toe 7

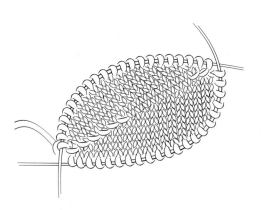

Short Row Toe 8

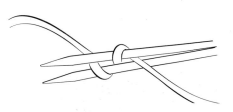

Figure Eight 1

Wrap the next stitch (so that it now has two wraps) and turn (see Short Row Toe 5).

Row 2 Slip the first (double-wrapped) stitch and purl across to the first unworked, wrapped stitch. Pick up the wrap and purl it together with the wrapped stitch. Wrap the next stitch and turn (see Short Row Toe 6).

On subsequent rows, you will pick up both wraps and knit or purl them together with the stitch.

Continue until you have worked all the stitches and you once again have 24 live stitches.

(If you are using double-pointed needles, divide the 24 stitches over 2 needles.)

Undo the bound-off end of your crocheted chain. Stick the point of a third double-pointed needle (or a second circular needle) in the stitch below the chain. Unzip the chain (like opening a bag of sugar) one stitch at a time as you stick the tip of the needle in each stitch, moving each stitch onto the needle (see Short Row Toe 7).

These stitches go on your second circular needle. If you are using double-pointed needles, divide these 24 stitches over the third and fourth needles (see Short Row Toe 8).

On your first round after toe shaping, you may want to pick up an extra stitch or two between the live stitches and the stitches you have picked up from the cast-on, to close up any holes that might have been created. On the next round, remember to decrease back down to the previous number of stitches per needle.

You will now continue knitting the foot of your sock.

FIGURE-EIGHT TOE

This toe can be a little tricky at the start, but you can easily master it with a bit of practice. One advantage is that you don't need a provisional cast-on or waste yarn. It's an easy technique to memorize, so you can do it "on the go," without having instructions in front of you every time.

Hold two circular needles with the points parallel. Hold the tail of the yarn against the front of the bottom needle, and bring the yarn from the front to the back between the needles, wrap it up and over from behind the top needle, then down in front of the top needle and between the needles again, from front to back, and around the bottom needle. You are wrapping your yarn around the needles in a figure eight (see Figure Eight 1).

Figure Eight 2

If your goal is to have, for example, a total of 16 stitches, you want to have 8 loops on each needle (see Figure Eight 2)

The working yarn is going between the needles from front to back, and the last loop is over the bottom needle. Turn your work upside down so what was the bottom needle is now on the top. Pull what is now the bottom needle out carefully so that the bottom stitches dangle on the cable of the needle.

Figure Eight 3

Using the free end of the top circular needle, knit the 8 stitches on that needle (see Figure Eight 3).

Now turn the work again so that the bottom needle with the unworked loops is now on top. Making sure to hold your working yarn tight and using the other end of the top circular needle, knit the 8 stitches on the top needle. For this initial row, the stitches will be twisted the wrong way, so you will need to knit into the backs of the loops when you encounter these twisted stitches (see Figure Eight 4).

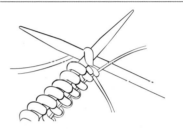

Figure Eight 4

Work 2 more rows like this so that you have completed 4 rows. You will have a needle at the top of your work with 8 stitches on it and a needle at the bottom of your work with 8 stitches on it (see Figure Eight 5).

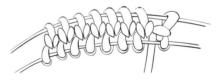

Figure Eight 5

You have completed the setup for your toe. The stitches in the middle of your work may be loose, but you can tighten them up a little by working the excess yarn toward one side after you have completed a couple of rounds.

Start the increases. Work the first round as follows:

Needle 1 K1, M1, knit to the last stitch, M1, k1.

Needle 2 K1, M1, knit to the last stitch, M1, k1.

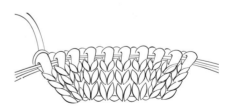

Figure Eight 6

Knit 1 round without increasing (see Figure Eight 6).

Repeat these 2 rounds until you have the total number of stitches you need for your sock, half on needle 1 and half on needle 2 (see Figure Eight 7).

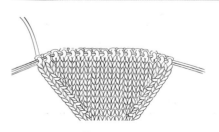

Figure Eight 7

Easy Toe 1

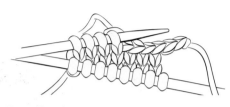

Easy Toe 2

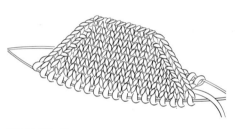

Easy Toe 3

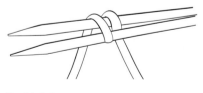

Turkish 1

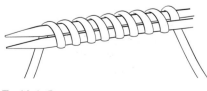

Turkish 2

"EASY" TOE

After you get past the cast-on, the construction of the "Easy Toe" is very similar to the Figure-Eight Toe but, as the name suggests, it is much easier. You will start with a provisional cast-on, like the Short-Row Toe. Using waste yarn, crochet a chain that is several chain stitches longer than the number of knit stitches you need. For example, if you are starting with 8 knit stitches, make your chain 12 stitches long. Cast off the last stitch and cut the yarn. Tie a knot in this tail of yarn; you are going to "unzip" this provisional cast-on later by undoing and pulling on this end, so the knot will make the right end easier to find.

Using your sock yarn and 1 circular needle or 2 double-pointed needles, knit 1 stitch into the bump in the center of each little V on the back side of the chain until you have 8 stitches (see Easy Toe 1).

Work in stockinette stitch for 4 rows. Unzip your provisional cast-on stitches, and place them on a second double-pointed needle or circular needle (see Easy Toe 2).

You will have a needle at the top of your work with 8 stitches on it and a needle at the bottom of your work with 8 stitches on it.

Start the increases. Work the first round as follows:

Needle 1 K1, M1, knit until the last stitch, M1, k1.

Needle 2 K1, M1, knit until the last stitch, M1, k1.

Knit 1 round without increasing.

Repeat these 2 rounds until you have the total number of stitches you need for your sock, half on needle 1 and half on needle 2 (see Easy Toe 3).

TURKISH CAST-ON

For the Turkish Cast-On, you will need two circular needles of the same size. They can be different lengths, however.

Make a slipknot on the top needle.

Holding the needles in your right hand with the points together, facing left, wrap the working yarn around both needles, working left to right, half the number of times that you want the total number of stitches to be (see Turkish 1).

For example, do 8 wraps for a total of 16 stitches. (Do not count the slipknot on the top needle.) (See Turkish 2.)

Turn your work upside down so what was the bottom needle is now on the top, and pull the bottom needle out until the wrapped loops are sitting in the middle of the cable of the needle; allow this bottom needle to dangle.

Bring the nonworking end of the top needle up to knit into the loops on the top needle (see Turkish 3).

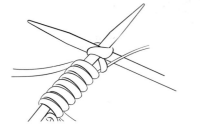

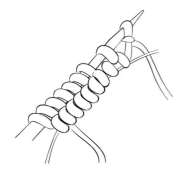

Turkish 3

After knitting the loops on the top needle, turn your work upside down. Slide the loops on the cable of what is now the top needle onto the tip of that needle, and slide the stitches just worked on the cable of what is now the bottom needle.

At this point, slide the slipknot off the tip of the needle and undo it, allowing it to hang (see Turkish 4).

Turkish 4

With the working yarn, which is coming from the last stitch on the other needle, knit across the loops with this needle. Be sure to pull the yarn snug as you work the first stitch, to avoid a gap (see Turkish 5).

Pull the needle through to the right so that the stitches just worked are on the cable and the needle is dangling. Turn. Slide the stitches to the tip of the now top needle, and knit across the stitches with the other end of this needle.

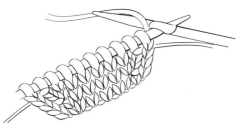

Turkish 5

After 2 rounds worked in this manner, start the increases. Work the first round as follows:

Needle 1 K1, M1, knit until the last stitch, M1, k1.

Needle 2 K1, M1, knit until the last stitch, M1, k1.

Then knit 1 round without increasing (see Turkish 6).

Repeat these 2 rounds until you have the total number of stitches you need for your sock, half on needle 1 and half on needle 2 (see Turkish 7).

Turkish 6

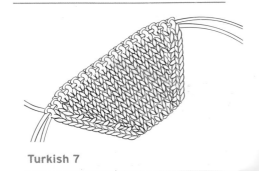

Turkish 7

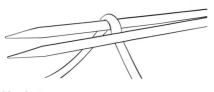

Magic 1

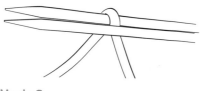

Magic 2

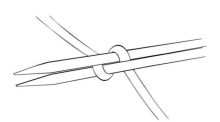

Magic 3

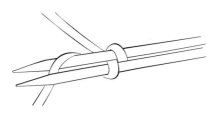

Magic 4

JUDY'S MAGIC CAST-ON

Judy's Magic Cast-On is my favorite cast-on method for toe-up socks. Once you get the hang of this technique, it is quick and easy to execute and makes a perfect toe every time. Its creator, Judy Becker, very generously gave me permission to share this technique here.

While I find that the easiest way to work this cast-on is with two circular needles, Judy shows you how to do it using double-pointed needles on her website (see the resources section, page 125).

You will need two circular needles of the same size. They can be different lengths, however.

Hold the two needles together in your right hand, one on top of the other.

Pull out some yarn from your skein. How much you pull out depends on how many stitches you are casting on. For a total of 16 stitches—8 on the top needle and 8 on the bottom needle—pull out about a 12" (30.5cm) tail of yarn.

Loop the yarn around the top needle so that the working yarn (the strand attached to the skein) is coming up from the bottom and the tail is in the back (see Magic 1).

With your left hand, pick up the yarn so that the tail goes over your index finger and the working yarn goes over your thumb.

Grasp both strands of yarn with the rest of your fingers to hold the yarn in place on the needle.

This will make a loop around the top needle that counts as 1 stitch (see Magic 2).

While holding the bottom strand firmly with your thumb, use your index finger to loop the yarn tail around the lower needle and pull it snug. You now have a loop (a stitch) on each needle (see Magic 3).

Now, while holding the yarn tail firmly with your index finger, bring the working yarn up with your thumb to loop around the top needle. There are now 2 stitches on the top needle: the loop you just cast on plus the first loop (see Magic 4).

You will continue in this manner, casting on loops by alternating between the index finger and the thumb. The yarn tail controlled by your index finger always wraps around the bottom needle, and the working yarn strand controlled by your thumb always wraps around the top needle.

Repeat these steps until you have cast on 8 stitches (or your desired number of stitches) onto each needle, for a total of 16 stitches (see Magic 5).

Now begin knitting these stitches:

Round 1 Turn the needles so that the bottom needle is now on the top. Pull the now bottom needle out until the stitches are sitting in the middle of the cable, and allow this needle to dangle. Pick up the working yarn. Make sure that the yarn tail is situated between the working yarn and the needle; otherwise, your first stitch will unravel.

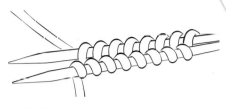

Magic 5

While holding the yarn tail snug with your left hand, knit the row of stitches. If the first stitch becomes loose while you are knitting it, you can pull on the yarn tail to tighten it up (see Magic 6).

Turn the work so that the working yarn is on the right and the needle with the unworked stitches is on the top. Pull the now bottom needle to the right so that the stitches you just knit are resting in the middle of the cable, and allow this needle to dangle. Pull the top needle to the left so that its stitches are ready to knit. Knit these stitches. Note that these stitches will be twisted so that on this first round only, you have to knit them through the back loops to reorient them so that they are sitting normally on the needle for the next round (see Magic 7).

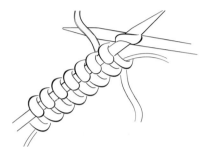

Magic 6

You have completed 1 round (see Magic 8).

You might find that the stitches are slightly uneven and loose. Remember to cast on over the needles at your usual cast-on gauge. Practice will make perfect. It may take you a few tries to get the hang of the perfect gauge.

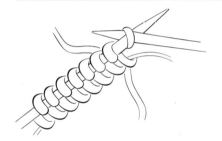

Magic 7

You are now ready to work your increases. Work the first round as follows:

Needle 1 K1, M1, knit until the last stitch, M1, k1.

Needle 2 K1, M1, knit until the last stitch, M1, k1.

Then knit 1 round without increasing.

Repeat these 2 rounds until you have the total number of stitches you need for your sock, half on needle 1 and half on needle 2 (see Magic 9).

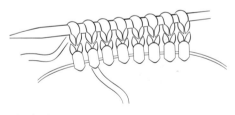

Magic 8

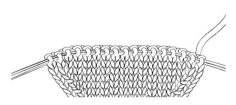

Magic 9

TECHNIQUES FOR KNITTING SOCKS ON DIFFERENT TYPES OF NEEDLES

THERE ARE A FEW DIFFERENT NEEDLE OPTIONS FOR KNITTING SOCKS. THEY ALL HAVE THEIR MERITS, AND YOU MAY FIND ONE MORE COMFORTABLE OR EASIER TO WORK WITH THAN THE OTHERS.

KNITTING A SOCK ON DOUBLE-POINTED NEEDLES

As discussed earlier, to knit socks on a set of five double-pointed needles, you will arrange your stitches over four of the needles and use the fifth needle to knit the stitches off one needle to the other. While it is possible to knit socks on four needles (stitches arranged over three and knit with the fourth), it is easier to make a sock on five, with the instep stitches evenly divided over two needles and the sole stitches over the other two. This stitch arrangement is less likely to cause a column of loose stitches at the juncture of the needles because the fewer needles, the more strain is placed at these points.

To get started knitting a sock using five double-pointed needles, you will first create a toe using one of the techniques described earlier. Note that some of these techniques are much easier to execute using two circular needles. Until you are comfortable using double-pointed needles, you can make your toe on two circular needles and then switch to double-pointed needles.

Arrange your stitches over four of the five needles (see DPN 1).

Pick up your work so that the start of your round is on the first needle in your left hand and the end of the round is on the last needle in your right hand.

Using the fifth double-pointed needle (the one that you did not put any stitches on), work the first stitch on the left needle as desired. Pull the yarn tight to avoid a hole (see DPN 2).

Continue to work the stitches on the left needle. When all the stitches are worked off the left needle, that one will become the free needle.

Now use the newly free needle to work the stitches on the next needle.

Continue working until you come to the end of the round.

TIP: MIND THE GAP!

Do you have ladders in your sock—a column of loose stitches that appear at the juncture of two needles? This commonly occurs when you knit in the round using double-pointed needles or two circulars.

To get rid of ladders, work the first stitch on your double-pointed needle as normal. As you work the second stitch, pull the working yarn tight before wrapping. This will adjust the tension on your first stitch and close up that pesky gap!

KNITTING A SOCK ON TWO CIRCULAR NEEDLES

Begin by dividing your stitches over the two needles: instep stitches on one needle and sole/heel stitches on the other (see Two Circs 1).

With your work facing you, slide the stitches to the right-hand point of the needle. Start knitting by working these with the needle point that is on the other end of that same circular needle (see Two Circs 2).

Knit until you have worked all the stitches on the first circular needle. Slide the worked stitches down onto the needle's cable, and turn the work so the other needle is in front.

Now work the stitches on the second needle. Slide the stitches to the right-hand point of the needle so that the first stitch is at the working end of the needle. Knit the first stitch firmly to tighten up any gap between the two needles.

KNITTING A SOCK ON ONE LONG CIRCULAR NEEDLE (THE MAGIC LOOP TECHNIQUE)

Divide the stitches so that half are on one needle tip and half are on the other needle tip. The stitches you are going to start working are on the front needle, and the needle cable is looped on the left side of the work, as you are facing it (see Magic Loop 1).

Pull the back needle tip out to the right so that the stitches slide onto the cable. Pull it out far enough so that you can easily use the back needle tip to knit the front stitches. You now have a loop of cable on each side of your work (see Magic Loop 2).

When you have worked all the stitches on the front needle (half the round has been completed), turn the work around and return the stitches to the position shown in the first illustration. The stitches you're about to knit are in front (closest to you), and the working yarn is on the right side of the needle in back.

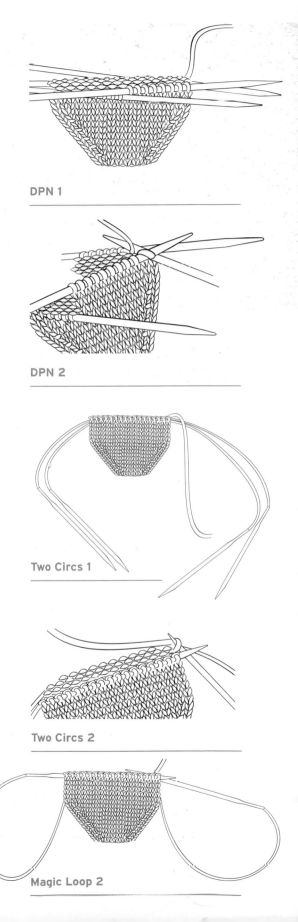

DPN 1

DPN 2

Two Circs 1

Two Circs 2

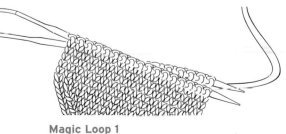

Magic Loop 1

Magic Loop 2

TECHNIQUES FOR CREATING HEELS

THERE ARE A NUMBER OF DIFFERENT HEEL STYLES YOU CAN USE FOR YOUR SOCKS. MY THREE FAVORITE HEELS FOR TOE-UP SOCKS ARE SHOWN HERE.

SHORT-ROW HEEL

The short-row heel (see Short-Row Heel) is, to my eye, the heel that looks most like a commercially produced sock. Because there is no gusset involved, however, this heel might not be the best choice for a foot with a very high instep—there is no extra ease in that area.

The short-row heel is worked exactly like the short-row toe with one exception. Instead of starting with a crocheted chain and working a provisional cast-on, you already have live stitches to begin with. You will work the heel over half the total stitches for the sock. Place these stitches on one needle. On the first row, knit across the heel stitches until 1 stitch remains unworked. With the yarn in front, slip the last stitch from the left needle to the right needle. Turn your work. On the second row, slip the first, un-worked stitch from the left needle to the right needle. Purl the next stitch (you will have wrapped that first stitch around its base with the working yarn), and purl across the next stitches in the row until 1

stitch remains unworked. With the yarn in front, slip the last stitch and turn.

Continue in this manner working 1 less stitch on each subsequent row until you have the number of live stitches you want in the center of the heel. Now you will work the second half of the heel, picking up 1 stitch and its wraps at the end of every row until all the heel stitches are live again.

After you have completed the heel, you will resume knitting in the round on all stitches.

A plain sock pattern with step-by-step instructions for the short-row heel sock is included in the patterns section on page 34.

GUSSET HEEL

This heel (see Gusset Heel) is worked by first creating a gusset by increasing on every other round after you reach a certain point on the foot, approximately 2" to 2 1/2" (5cm–6.5cm) shy of the

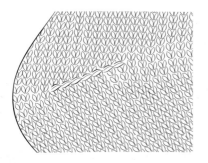

Short-Row Heel

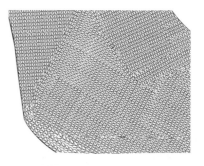

Gusset Heel

desired total length of the foot. After you have completed the increases, you work in short rows, decreasing 1 stitch at the end of each short row until you have decreased back down to your original stitch count.

The resulting heel is nice and smooth and easy to work. I like to use this heel for sportweight socks because it doesn't add the extra bit of bulk that comes with the slip stitch heel. Extra thickness in heavier socks can be very uncomfortable.

A plain sock pattern with step-by-step instructions for the gusset heel is included in the patterns section on page 38.

SLIP STITCH HEEL

This heel (see Slip Stitch Heel) is worked in a manner similar to the gusset heel. First, you create a gusset by increasing on every other round after you reach a certain point on the foot, approximately 3" (7.5cm) shy of the desired total length of the foot. When you have completed the increases, you work some short rows to form the curve of the back of the heel. Then you work across short rows, slipping alternate stitches and decreasing 1 stitch at the end of each short row until you have decreased back down to your original stitch count. This heel looks exactly like a traditional slip stitch heel sock that is worked from the top down.

A plain sock pattern with step-by-step instructions for the slip stitch heel is included in the patterns section on page 40.

TIP: MAKING A NEAT GUSSET INCREASE

For my gusset increases, I prefer to knit in the front and back of a stitch. I find that it makes an attractive increase and leaves no holes in the knitted fabric. Make the increase inside each edge stitch of the gusset. For example, if you are creating a gusset across 32 stitches, you will work as follows:

On the first increase row, kf&b, k29, kf&b, k1. You now have 34 stitches.

On the second increase row, kf&b, k31, kf&b, k1. You now have 36 stitches.

TIP: HOW TO AVOID HOLES AT THE TOP OF THE HEEL

Because the heel of a sock is worked back and forth on half the total stitches, the gap between the instep and sole stitches will often stretch a bit from the stress put on it during the heel-turning process (see Hole 1).

After you have completed a heel and you are ready to start knitting in the round again, you can pick up 1 or 2 extra stitches at the juncture of the heel and instep stitches on the first round. Then, on the second round, decrease back down to the proper number of stitches. If you forget to do this and there is a hole at that point, you can always tighten up the stitches with a bit of yarn and a tapestry needle after the sock is completed. Just be sure to fasten the yarn off securely on the wrong side. No one will ever know! (See Hole 2.)

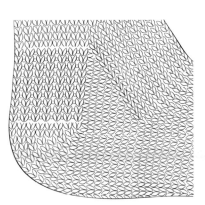

Slip Stitch Heel

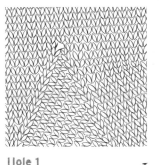

Hole 1　　　**Hole 2**

BIND-OFFS

JUST AS THERE ARE MANY WAYS TO CAST ON FOR TOE-UP SOCKS, THERE ARE MANY WAYS TO BIND OFF THE CUFFS. A FEW OF MY FAVORITE TECHNIQUES ARE EXPLAINED HERE.

SEWN BIND-OFF

The sewn bind-off is quick and easy to do, which makes it one of my favorites. When you work it, be sure not to pull the yarn too tight through the stitches. You want the edge to be nice and stretchy. What might look somewhat ruffled and unattractive with the sock off the leg looks smooth when the sock is worn.

When you have finished knitting the cuff of your sock, cut the yarn, leaving a tail at least 18" (45.5cm) long and thread it through a tapestry needle.

First, insert the yarn through the first 2 stitches on the needle as if to purl, and gently pull all the way through. Leave these stitches on the needle (see Sewn 1).

Now, insert the yarn back through the first stitch on the needle as if to knit, and gently pull it all the way through, dropping that stitch off the needle (see Sewn 2).

Repeat these two steps until you have sewn through all of the stitches. Weave the end of the yarn tail invisibly on the inside of the sock, and trim the end (see Sewn 3).

TIP: HIDING BIND-OFFS

It's easy to make the point between the beginning and the end of the bind-off less discernible. After you run the yarn back through the first stitch, move it from the left needle to the right needle so that it will become the last stitch to be cast off.

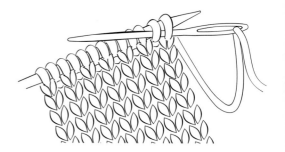

Sewn 1

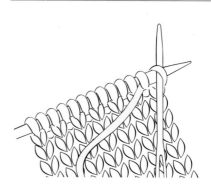

Sewn 2

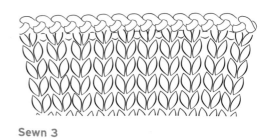

Sewn 3

RUSSIAN BIND-OFF

The Russian bind-off is another great favorite of mine because it, too, is quick and easy. It has the advantage of being executed without any tools other than your knitting needles. In some instructions for the Russian bind-off, you are told to work the bind-off in purl all the way around or in knit all the way around. When I am doing a ribbed cuff on a sock, I do the bind-off in ribbing. I generally do k2, p2 or k3, p3 ribbing, so I knit the knits and purl the purls. When it comes to working the 2 stitches together, I work it knit or purl, depending on what the second stitch of the two is, working the decrease as "knit 2 together through back loops" or "purl 2 together."

(In the instructions below, I use the word *work* to mean either knit or purl, depending on which stitch presents itself next.)

Work 2 and slip these 2 stitches back onto the left-hand needle, work 2 together (see Russian 1).

Now work 1 and slip the 2 stitches onto the right-hand needle back to the left-hand needle, work 2 together (see Russian 2).

Repeat the second step until you have 1 stitch remaining. Cut your yarn and fasten it off (see Russian 3).

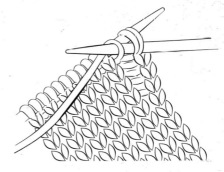

Russian 1

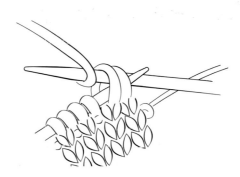

Russian 2

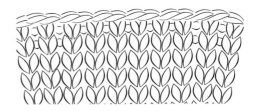

Russian 3

TUBULAR BIND-OFF

The tubular bind-off works when you are creating a k1, p1 ribbing. It involves a bit of extra work, as you first separate the knit and purl stitches onto two different needles and then graft the stitches together. It creates a beautiful stretchy edge. Trust me, it's worth the extra effort.

Work k1, p1 ribbing for the cuff of the sock, as deep as you want your cuff to be.

Now work 4 rounds as follows:

Round 1 Work k1 sl1 around.

Round 2 Work sl1 p1 around.

Round 3 As round 1.

Round 4 As round 2 (see Tubular 1).

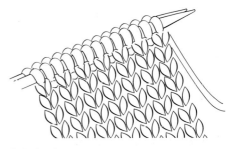

Tubular 1

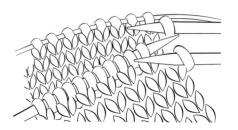

Tubular 2

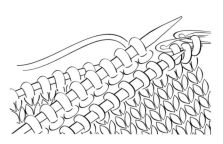

Tubular 3

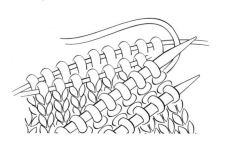

Tubular 4

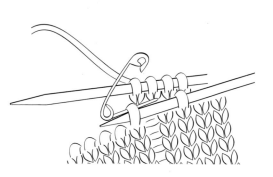

Tubular 5

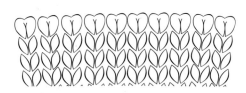

Tubular 6

You now need to separate the stitches. Hold two circular needles in your right hand. Slip the first knit stitch onto the front needle (simply transfer it from needle to needle; do not twist it). Slip the first purl stitch onto the back needle (again, simply transfer it from needle to needle without twisting). (See Tubular 2.)

Repeat for all stitches.

You now have all your knit stitches on the front needle and all your purl stitches on the back needle (see Tubular 3).

Now you need to graft the stitches together. Cut the yarn, leaving a tail of at least 18" (45.5cm) long, and thread it through a tapestry needle.

When you start grafting, on the first knit stitch insert the yarn through the stitch and pull it through, but place a coil-less pin through the stitch before you drop it off the needle. Repeat for the first purl stitch (see Tubular 4).

When you have finished grafting all the stitches in the round, put the pinned knit stitch back on the front needle and put the pinned purl stitch on the back needle (see Tubular 5).

Do the last half of the grafting maneuver on the final repeat (see Tubular 6).

TIP: HOW TO GRAFT

Grafting, or the "Kitchener stitch," is covered in the techniques section of most knitting how-to and reference books as well as in many online tutorials. Basically, you have the stitches to be grafted on parallel needles held in your left hand and the yarn tail threaded through a tapestry needle.

Set up to graft:

Insert the threaded tapestry needle into the first stitch on the needle closest to you as if to purl and pull it through, leaving the stitch on the needle.

Then insert the needle into the first stitch on the back needle as if to knit, leaving the stitch on the needle. Pull the yarn through.

Now perform the following four steps:

1. Insert the yarn through the first stitch on the front needle as if to knit, and slip the stitch off the end of the needle.

2. Insert the yarn through the next stitch on the front needle as if to purl, and leave it on the needle. Gently pull the yarn through the stitch.

3. Insert the yarn through the first stitch on the back needle as if to purl, and slip it off the end of the needle.

4. Insert the yarn through the next stitch on the back needle as if to knit, and leave it on the needle. Pull the yarn through the stitch.

You can chant a mantra while you do this: "front knit-off, front purl-on," and "back purl-off, back knit-on." It works for me!

PICOT EDGE

There are a few different ways to create a picot edge. This one is very easy, which makes it another favorite of mine.

Work 6 rounds in stockinette stitch (knit every stitch).

On the next round, k1, yo around to create a row of eyelets.

Work 6 more rounds for a facing and bind off very loosely (see Picot 1).

Using the yarn tail threaded through a tapestry needle, turn the facing to the inside of the sock, folding at the eyelet round, and loosely stitch down in place (see Picot 2).

Gently press the edge with a steam iron, or wet-block it (see Picot 3).

There are variations on the picot edge. You can leave the stitches "live" after completing the facing and tack each live stitch down by threading the yarn through each loop and through the back of a stitch on the inside of the sock. You can also work the facing in a k1, p1 ribbing to draw it in slightly to hug the leg.

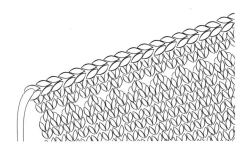

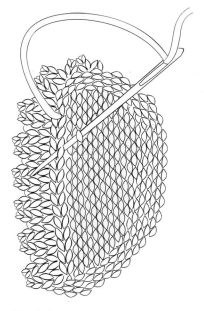

Picot 1

Picot 2

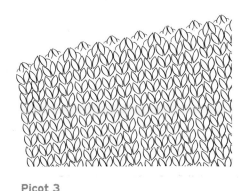

Picot 3

PART 2: SOCK PATTERNS

Most of the patterns here are written for working with either two circular needles or one long circular needle. In these patterns, the stitches are divided into two groups: instep stitches and sole stitches. You can easily work most of the patterns on double-pointed needles by dividing the stitches in each of the two sections over two double-pointed needles. In some of the patterns, the stitches will not divide evenly, because there is an odd number of stitches in each of the two sock halves. Using double-pointed needles for socks with one pattern chart repeat that covers the whole half of the sock will be more difficult.

HOW TALL DO YOU MAKE YOUR SOCKS?

All of the patterns here instruct you to knit your sock until it is the length you want in the leg. The yarn amounts given here are based on socks that are a woman's size medium to large and are 6" (15cm) or so in the leg above the heel.

In most of the patterns in this book, you will work a pattern on the instep stitches and work the sole stitches in plain stockinette stitch. However, after you turn the heel, you are sometimes directed to start working the pattern on the stitches above the heel so that the pattern is repeated all the way around the leg of the sock. When you start working in the round again after completing the heel, you will work the pattern from the chart on the back of the leg in the same manner as you are instructed to do on the front of the leg. If there is a small pattern repeat (2 or 4 rows), you might want to wait to begin working the chart pattern on the back of the sock with row 1. In that case, work plain stockinette stitch over the back stitches until you have reached row 1 of the pattern on the front stitches.

TIP: HOW TO WORK TWO IDENTICAL SOCKS

One way to make sure that your socks are identical is to knit two socks at a time on long circular needles or on two sets of needles, alternating working one round on one sock and then one round on the second sock. However, I prefer to knit my socks one at a time. I keep track of how many rounds I knit in the first sock and knit the identical number of rounds in the second sock. If you are knitting a sock with a multiple-row pattern repeat, this is easy.

When you get to the point where it is time to start working your gusset increases, make a note of how many complete pattern repeats you've worked and what numbered round in the pattern is the last round before you start the increases. Work the gusset and heel. Then work the leg of the sock as high as you want. Once again, make a note of how many pattern repeats you've worked and which pattern round you worked last if you are working a partial repeat before you start the ribbing or other top edge of the sock. By keeping track of these numbers, you can easily make your second sock identical to the first.

BASIC SOCKS

I'VE INCLUDED THREE "PLAIN VANILLA" PATTERNS HERE. EACH one uses one of the three heel techniques shown in the techniques section on pages 24-25. You can use them to practice your toe and heel techniques before embarking on one of the more complicated patterns. You can also use them to plug in your own stitch patterns to create your own designs. Do you have a particularly colorful or wildly variegated hand-painted sock yarn you want to use? One of these plain vanilla patterns is your best bet so that your sock pattern doesn't fight with all those colors.

SHORT-ROW TOE
AND HEEL BASIC SOCKS

SIZE: M (L), 8 (9)" (20.5 [23]cm)

GAUGE: 8 stitches and 12 rows = 1" (2.5cm) in stockinette stitch

NEEDLES: 1 set US size 0 (2mm) double-pointed needles, or size needed to obtain gauge

YARN: 1 skein Cherry Tree Hill Supersock Solids, 100% luxury merino fingering weight, 4 oz (113.5g), 420 yd (384m), Natural (1) Superfine

---

Note: This pattern is written using 64 stitches around for the sock, with adjustments for 72 stitches in parentheses, but you can adjust this pattern for any size, any gauge. Measure around the ball of your foot. Multiply the number of inches you get by the number of stitches you get per inch when you do a gauge swatch. Then subtract 10 percent from that total. Fudge your number so that it is divisible by 4. This will make a nice, snug-fitting sock.

SHORT-ROW TOE

Using a provisional cast-on, cast on 32 (36) stitches (half the total circumference of the sock).

Row 1 Knit 31 (35) stitches. Move the working yarn as if to purl. Slip the last, unworked stitch from the left needle onto the right needle. Turn your work.

Row 2 Slip the first, unworked stitch from the left needle onto the right needle. Purl the next stitch (you will have wrapped that first stitch around its base with the working yarn) and purl across to the last stitch. Move the working yarn as if to knit and slip the last stitch. Turn.

Row 3 Slip the first stitch and knit across to the last stitch before the unworked stitch. Wrap and turn.

Row 4 Slip the first stitch and purl across to the stitch before the unworked stitch. Wrap and turn. Repeat rows 3 and 4 until 9 (11) of the toe stitches are wrapped and on the left side, 14 (14) stitches are "live" in the middle, and 9 (11) are wrapped and on the right. At this stage, you should be ready to work a right-side row. Your toe is half done.

Note: How many stitches you leave unworked in the middle depends on how wide you want your sock toe to be. If you want it a bit wider, do a couple fewer short rows. If you want it a bit narrower, do a couple more short rows.

Now work the second half of the toe:

Row 1 Knit across the 14 live stitches to the first unworked, wrapped stitch. To work this stitch, pick up the wrap and knit it together with the stitch. Wrap the next stitch (so that it now has two wraps) and turn.

Row 2 Slip the first (double-wrapped) stitch and purl across to the first unworked, wrapped stitch. Pick up the wrap and purl it together with the stitch. Wrap the next stitch and turn.

On subsequent rows, you will pick up both wraps and knit or purl them together with the stitch. Continue until you have worked all the stitches and you once again have 32 (36) "live" stitches. When all 32 (36) stitches are once again "live," divide those stitches over 2 needles. Unzip your provisional cast-on and divide those 32 (36) stitches over 2 more needles. On your first round, you may want to pick up an extra stitch or two between the "live" stitches and the stitches you've picked up from the cast-on, to close up any holes that might have been created. On the next round, decrease back down to 16 (18) stitches per needle. You now have a total of 64 (72) stitches.

FOOT

Work even until the foot is about 2½" (6.5cm) shorter than the desired finished length. You will leave the 32 (36) instep stitches on 2 needles (you will not work on these stitches while you turn the heel) and move the 32 (36) heel stitches onto 1 needle. Work a short-row heel on the 32 (36) heel stitches as for the toe, as follows.

SHORT-ROW HEEL

Row 1 Knit 31 (35) stitches. Move the working yarn as if to purl. Slip the last, unworked stitch from the left needle onto the right needle. Turn.

Row 2 Slip the first, unworked stitch from the left needle onto the right needle. Purl the next stitch (you will have wrapped that first stitch around its base with the working yarn) and purl across to the last stitch. Move the working yarn as if to knit and slip the last stitch. Turn.

Row 3 Slip the first stitch and knit across to the last stitch before the unworked stitch. Wrap and turn.

Row 4 Slip the first stitch and purl across to the stitch before the unworked stitch. Wrap and turn. Repeat rows 3 and 4 until 9 (11) of the toe stitches are wrapped and on the left side, 14 (14) stitches are "live" in the middle, and 9 (11) are wrapped and on the right. At this stage, you should be ready to work a right-side row. Your heel is half finished.

Note: How many stitches you leave unworked in the middle depends on how wide you want your sock heel to be. If you want it a bit wider, do a couple fewer short rows. If you want it a bit narrower, do a couple more short rows.

Now work the second half of the heel:

Row 1 Knit across the 14 live stitches to the first unworked, wrapped stitch. To work this stitch, pick up the wrap and knit it together with the stitch. Wrap the next stitch (so that it now has two wraps) and turn.

Row 2 Slip the first (double-wrapped) stitch and purl across to the first unworked, wrapped stitch. Pick up the wrap and purl it together with the stitch. Wrap the next stitch and turn.

On subsequent rows, you will pick up both wraps and knit or purl them together with the stitch.

Continue until you have worked all of the stitches—32 (36) "live" stitches.

When you have all stitches live again, divide these 32 (36) stitches over 2 needles and begin working in the round again. On your first round, you may want to pick up an extra stitch or two between the "live" stitches and the stitches you left on a needle for the instep, to close up any holes that might be there. On the next round, remember to decrease back down to 16 (18) stitches per needle.

Now start working in the round again.

FINISHING

When your sock is 1" (2.5cm) short of the desired leg length, work in k1, p1 ribbing for 1" (2.5cm). Bind off very loosely in rib.

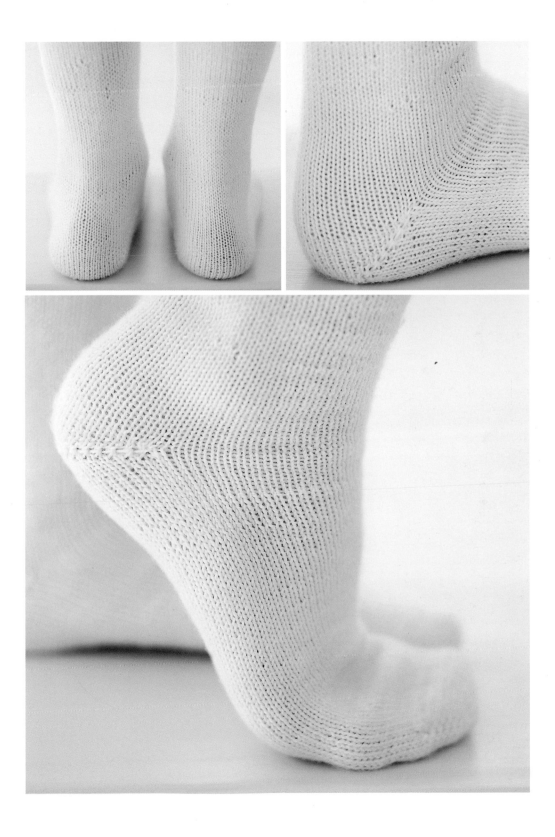

GUSSET HEEL BASIC SOCKS

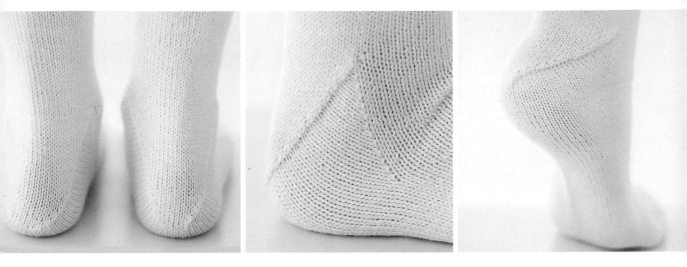

SIZE: M (L), 8 (9)" (20.5 [23]cm)

GAUGE: 8 stitches and 12 rows = 1" (2.5cm) in stockinette stitch

NEEDLES: 1 set US size 0 (2mm) double-pointed needles, or size needed to obtain gauge

YARN USED: 1 skein Cherry Tree Hill Supersock Solids, 100% luxury merino fingering weight, 4 oz (113.5g), 420 yd (384m), Natural ⬛1 Superfine

TOE

Using a Turkish Cast-On, Figure-Eight Cast-On, or Judy's Magic Cast-On (page 20), cast on 32 (36) stitches—16 (18) stitches on each needle. Knit across the stitches on each needle once. On the next round, increase 4 stitches as follows:

Needle 1 K1, M1, knit until the last stitch, M1, k1.

Needle 2 K1, M1, knit until the last stitch, M1, k1.

Then knit a round without increasing.

Repeat these 2 rounds until you have a total of 64 (72) stitches— 32 (36) stitches on each needle. Separate the stitches as follows:

Needle 1 (instep) 16 (18) stitches
Needle 2 (instep) 16 (18) stitches
Needle 3 (sole) 16 (18) stitches
Needle 4 (sole) 16 (18) stitches

Work the foot until you reach the point where your foot connects to the ankle, or approximately 2 to 2½" (5cm–6.5cm) shy of the total length of the sock.

CREATE THE GUSSET

Round 1 Knit across needle 1 and needle 2 (the instep stitches).

Needle 3 (sole stitches) K1, M1, knit across the remaining stitches.

Needle 4 (sole stitches) Knit across to the last stitch, M1, k1.

Round 2 Knit all stitches.

Repeat rounds 1 and 2 until you have 28 (30) stitches each on needles 3 and 4.

TURN THE HEEL

Slip all stitches from needles 3 and 4 onto 1 needle. You will work back and forth on these stitches and will not knit the stitches on needles 1 and 2 while turning the heel. Turn the heel as follows:

Row 1 K31 (35), ssk, k1, turn.
Row 2 Sl1, p7, p2tog, p1, turn.
Row 3 Sl1, k8, ssk, k1, turn.
Row 4 Sl1, p9, p2tog, p1, turn.
Row 5 Sl1, k10, ssk, k1, turn.
Row 6 Sl1, p11, p2tog, p1, turn.

Continue in this manner until all of the stitches are worked and you have 32 (34) stitches on the needle. Divide these 32 (34) stitches over 2 needles and resume working in the round. Work the leg in stockinette stitch until it is 1" (2.5cm) shy of the desired leg length.

FINISHING

Work k2, p2 ribbing for 1" (2.5cm).

SLIP STITCH HEEL BASIC SOCKS

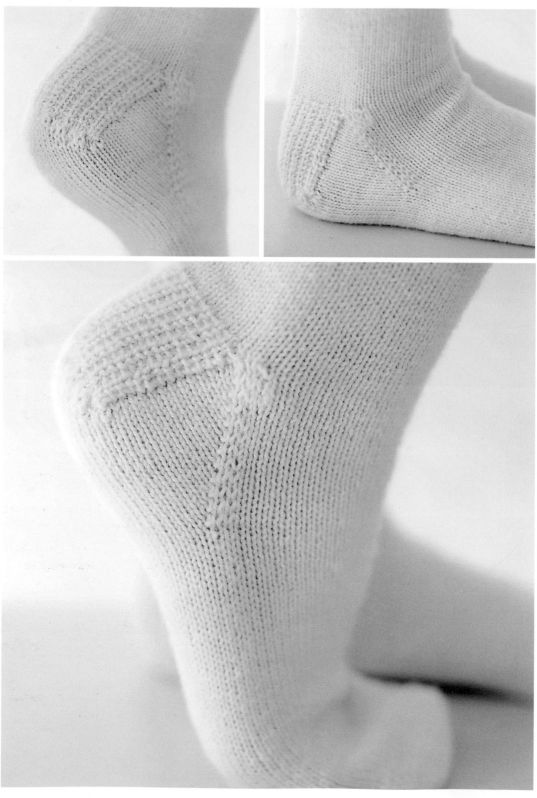

SIZE: M (L), 8¼ (9¼)" (21 [23.5]cm)

GAUGE: 8 stitches and 12 rows = 1" (2.5cm) in stockinette stitch

NEEDLES: 2 US size 0 (2mm) circular needles (or 1 long circular needle), or size needed to obtain gauge

YARN USED: 2 skeins Shibui Knits Sock, 100% superwash merino wool, 1¾ oz (50g), 191 yd (174.5m), Ivory (color number 7501) ⓵ Superfine

---

TOE

Using a Turkish Cast-On, Figure-Eight Cast-On, or Judy's Magic Cast-On (page 20), cast on a total of 30 (34) stitches—15 (17) stitches on each needle. Knit across the stitches on each needle once. On the next round, increase 4 stitches as follows:

Needle 1 K1, M1, knit until the last stitch, M1, k1.

Needle 2 K1, M1, knit until the last stitch, M1, k1.

Then knit a round without increasing.

Repeat these 2 rounds until you have a total of 66 (74) stitches—33 (37) stitches on each needle.

Note: If you prefer a pointier toe, you can cast on fewer stitches, but be sure to increase until you have 33 (37) stitches on each of the 2 needles.

Work in stockinette stitch until approximately 3" (7.5cm) shy of the total length of the foot.

GUSSET

Round 1 Knit across needle 1. Needle 2 (sole stitches): K1, M1, knit across to the last stitch, M1, k1.

Round 2 Knit across needle 1. Needle 2 (sole stitches): Knit all stitches.

Repeat rounds 1 and 2 until you have a total of 55 (61) stitches on needle 2.

TURN THE HEEL

Knit across needle 1. You will now work back and forth on the stitches on needle 2 and will not work the stitches on needle 1 while turning the heel.

Turn the heel as follows:

Row 1 (RS) K37 (41), kf&b, k1, w&t.

Row 2 P22 (24), pf&b, p1, w&t.

Row 3 K20 (22), kf&b, k1, w&t.

Row 4 P18 (20), pf&b, p1, w&t.

Row 5 K16 (18), kf&b, k1, w&t.

Row 6 P14 (16), pf&b, p1, w&t.

Row 7 K12 (14), kf&b, k1, w&t.

Row 8 P10 (12), pf&b, p1, w&t.

Needle 2 now holds 63 (69) stitches, having just completed a wrong-side row. On the right side, knit to the end of needle 2, knitting each wrap together with the stitch it wraps. Knit across the instep stitches on needle 1.

HEEL FLAP

Work back and forth on the heel stitches on needle 2:

Row 1 (RS) K47 (52) (knitting each wrap together with the stitch it wraps), ssk, turn.

Row 2 Sl1, p31 (35), p2tog, turn.

Row 3 *Sl1, k1; repeat from * 16 (18) times, ssk, turn.

Repeat rows 2 and 3 until all of the side stitches have been worked, and end after having worked row 2. Needle 2 now holds 33 (37) stitches.

Begin working in the round again, knitting all stitches around the sock.

Continue in this manner, working until the leg of the sock is 1" (2.5cm) shy of the desired length.

FINISHING

Work 1" (2.5cm) in k1, p1 ribbing. Bind off loosely in rib.

LACE SOCKS

SOCKS ARE A GREAT PLACE TO SHOWCASE LACE PATTERNS, and lace lends itself particularly well to socks. Most lace makes for a stretchy fabric, so the socks are forgiving and will fit a variety of feet. Are you a lace newbie and a little scared? Don't be! It's just yarn overs and decreases. The Dead Simple Lace Socks (page 44), Lacy Ribs Socks (page 48), Diagonal Lace Socks (page 51), and Tic-Tac-Toe-Up Socks (page 54) all have very simple lace motifs, with logical repeats and few stitches and rows per motif. They are perfect for new lace knitters or for anyone who wants to knit pretty socks without having to pay attention too closely.

The intermediate lace socks patterns—Butterfly Socks (page 57), On-Hold Socks (page 60), Ribbed Ribbons Socks (page 64), and Trilobite Socks (page 68)—are slightly more challenging, but don't let that deter you. The lace motifs are bigger and may encompass more rows, but you are still simply doing yarn overs and decreases. Just pay attention to where you are in the pattern, and you'll be fine.

The advanced lace sock patterns—Hearts and Flowers Socks (page 72), Lace and Cable Socks (page 76), Riding on the Metro Socks (page 80), and Sheri's Posies Socks (page 84)—will challenge you a bit, but like the intermediate patterns, if you pay attention you'll have no problems at all. The motifs are large and encompass 16 to 32 rows. The results, I think, are well worth the effort!

DEAD SIMPLE LACE SOCKS

THIS A GOOD PLACE FOR THE LACE NOVICE TO BEGIN. USING YARNOVERS AND SLANTED DECREASES ON A PLAIN STOCKINETTE BACKGROUND RESULTS IN A LOVELY SOCK YOU WILL BE PROUD TO WEAR OR GIVE AS A GIFT. BECAUSE THE PATTERN IS SO SIMPLE, YOU CAN USE A SOMEWHAT VARIEGATED YARN AND GET PLEASING RESULTS.

SIZE: M (L), 8½ (9½)" (21.5 [24]cm)

GAUGE: 8 stitches and 12 rows = 1" (2.5cm) in stockinette stitch

NEEDLES: 1 set US size 0 (2mm) double-pointed needles, or size needed to obtain gauge

YARN USED: 1 skein Lisa Souza Sock! Merino, 100% superfine merino superwash, 4 oz (113.5g), 560 yd (512m), Printemps ⬛ Superfine

Note: This pattern is written with a short-row toe and heel, but you could easily adapt it to other toe and heel styles.

SHORT-ROW TOE

Using a provisional cast-on, cast on 32 (36) stitches (half the total circumference of the sock).

Row 1 Knit 31 (35) stitches. Move the working yarn as if to purl. Slip the last, unworked stitch from the left needle onto the right needle. Turn your work.

Row 2 Slip the first, unworked stitch from the left needle onto the right needle. Purl the next stitch (you will have wrapped that first stitch around its base with the working yarn) and purl across to the last stitch. Move the working yarn as if to knit and slip the last stitch. Turn.

Row 3 Slip the first stitch and knit across to the last stitch before the unworked stitch. Wrap and turn.

Row 4 Slip the first stitch and purl across to the stitch before the unworked stitch. Wrap and turn.

Repeat rows 3 and 4 until 9 (11) of the toe stitches are wrapped and on left side, 14 (14) stitches are "live" in the middle, and 9 (11) stitches are wrapped and on the right. At this stage, you should be ready to work a right-side row. Your toe is half done.

Note: How many stitches you leave unworked in the middle depends on how wide you want your sock toe to be. If you want it a bit wider, do a couple fewer short rows. If you want it a bit narrower, do a couple more short rows.

Now work the second half of the toe:

Row 1 Knit across the 14 live stitches to the first unworked, wrapped stitch. To work this stitch, pick up the wrap and knit it together with the stitch. Wrap the next stitch (so that it now has two wraps) and turn.

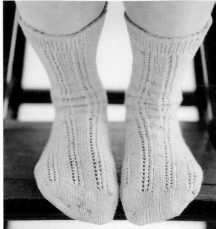

DEAD SIMPLE LACE SOCKS (CONTINUED)

Row 2 Slip the first (double-wrapped) stitch and purl across to the first unworked, wrapped stitch. Pick up the wrap and purl it together with the stitch. Wrap the next stitch and turn.

On subsequent rows, you will pick up both wraps and knit or purl them together with the stitch. Continue until you have worked all of the stitches and you once again have 32 (36) "live" stitches. When all 32 (36) stitches are once again "live," divide those stitches over 2 needles. Unzip your provisional cast-on and divide those 32 (36) stitches over 2 more needles. On your first round, you may want to pick up an extra stitch or two between the "live" stitches and the stitches you've picked up from the cast-on, to close up any holes that might be there. On the next round, remember to decrease back down to 16 (18) stitches per needle. You now have a total of 64 (72) stitches.

Start the lace pattern:
Needles 1 and 2 hold the instep stitches, and needles 3 and 4 hold the sole stitches. Work the lace pattern over needles 1 and 2, and knit all the stitches on needles 3 and 4.

Work even until the foot is approximately 2½" (6.5cm) shorter than the desired finished length. Leave the 32 (36) instep stitches on 2 needles (you will not work on these stitches while you turn the heel), and move the 32 (36) heel stitches onto 1 needle. Work a short-row heel on the 32 (36) heel stitches as for the toe, as follows.

SHORT-ROW HEEL
Row 1 Knit 31 (35) stitches. Move the working yarn as if to purl. Slip the last, unworked stitch from the left needle to the right needle. Turn your work.
Row 2 Slip the first, unworked stitch from the left needle onto the right needle. Purl the next

stitch (you will have wrapped that first stitch around its base with the working yarn) and purl across to the last stitch. Move the working yarn as if to knit and slip the last stitch. Turn.
Row 3 Slip the first stitch and knit across to the last stitch before the unworked stitch. Wrap and turn.
Row 4 Slip the first stitch and purl across to the stitch before the unworked stitch. Wrap and turn.
Repeat rows 3 and 4 until 9 (11) of the toe stitches are wrapped and on the left side, 14 (14) stitches are "live" in the middle, and 9 (11) stitches are wrapped and on the right. At this stage, you should be ready to work a right-side row. Your heel is half done.

Note: How many stitches you leave unworked in the middle depends on how wide you want your sock heel to be. If you want it a bit wider, do a couple fewer short rows. If you want it a bit narrower, do a couple more short rows.

Now work the second half of the heel:

Row 1 Knit across the 14 live stitches to the first unworked, wrapped stitch. To work this stitch, pick up the wrap and knit it together with the stitch. Wrap the next stitch (so that it now has two wraps) and turn.

Row 2 Slip the first (double-wrapped) stitch and purl across to the first unworked, wrapped stitch. Pick up the wrap and purl it together with the stitch. Wrap the next stitch and turn.

On subsequent rows you will pick up both wraps and knit or purl them together with the stitch.

Continue until you have worked all of the stitches and you once again have 32 (36) "live" stitches. When you have all stitches live again, divide these 32 (36) stitches over 2 needles and begin working in the round again. On your first round, you may want to pick up an extra stitch or two between the "live" stitches and the stitches you left on a needle for the instep, to close up any holes that might be there. On the next round, remember to decrease back down to 16 (18) stitches per needle. You will now start working the lace pattern on the stitches on

needles 3 and 4. Work 1 repeat of the pattern over needles 3 and 4, ensuring that you are starting in the right place on the chart so that it corresponds with the chart on needles 1 and 2.

FINISHING
When your sock is 1" (2.5cm) short of the desired leg length, work in k1, p1 ribbing for 1" (2.5cm). Bind off very loosely in rib.

DEAD SIMPLE LACE SOCKS

key

	K
/	K2TOG
\	SSK
O	YO

lace chart large

| 35 | 33 | 31 | 29 | 27 | 25 | 23 | 21 | 19 | 17 | 15 | 13 | 11 | 9 | 7 | 5 | 3 | 1 |

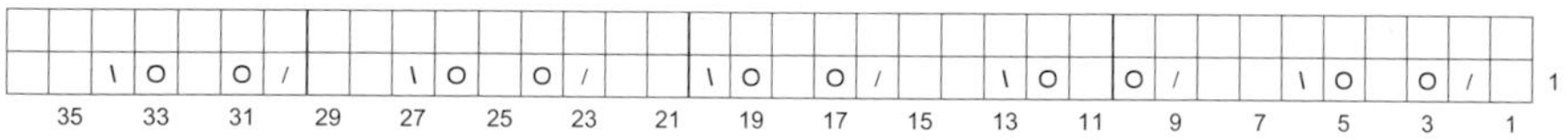

lace chart medium

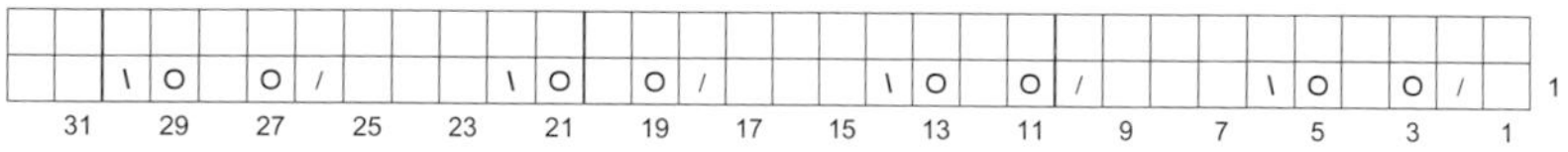

| 31 | 29 | 27 | 25 | 23 | 21 | 19 | 17 | 15 | 13 | 11 | 9 | 7 | 5 | 3 | 1 |

LACY RIBS SOCKS

THIS PATTERN IS A GREAT CHOICE FOR ALL THOSE HAND-PAINTED SOCK YARNS YOU HAVE IN YOUR STASH—IT LOOKS GOOD IN SOLIDS OR PATTERNS, AND IN STRIPES OR POOLS. IT FEATURES A LACE MOTIF THAT YOU CAN EASILY MEMORIZE. IT'S ALSO VERY STRETCHY.

SIZE: S (M, L), 7¼ (8¼, 9¼)" (18.5cm [21, 23.5]cm)

GAUGE: 8 stitches and 12 rows = 1" (2.5cm) in stockinette stitch

NEEDLES: 2 US size 0 (2mm) circular needles (or 1 long circular needle), or size needed to obtain gauge

YARN USED: 2 skeins Fiesta Baby Boomerang, extra fine superwash merino, 2 oz (56.5g), 220 yd (201m), Dreamsicle 🔘 Superfine

---

TOE

Using a Turkish Cast-On, Figure-Eight Cast-On, or Judy's Magic Cast-On (page 20), cast on a total of 28 (32, 36) stitches—14 (16, 18) stitches on each needle. Knit across the stitches on each needle once. On the next round, increase 4 stitches as follows:

Needle 1 K1, M1, knit until the last stitch, M1, k1.

Needle 2 K1, M1, knit until the last stitch, M1, k1.

Then knit a round without increasing.

Repeat these 2 rounds until you have a total of 56 (64, 72) stitches—28 (32, 36) stitches on each needle.

Start the lace pattern:

You will work the chart over needle 1 only (the instep stitches) and knit across the stitches on needle 2.

Work 7 (8, 9) repeats of the lace pattern over needle 1; knit all the stitches on needle 2.

Continue in this manner, working as many repeats of the 4-row chart as necessary until your work measures approximately 3" (7.5cm) shy of the total length of the foot.

CREATE THE GUSSET

Round 1 Work across needle 1 in the lace pattern. Needle 2 (sole stitches): K1, M1, knit across to the last stitch, M1, k1.

Round 2 Work across needle 1 in the lace pattern. Needle 2 (sole stitches): Knit all stitches.

Repeat rounds 1 and 2 until you have 48 (54, 60) stitches total on needle 2. On the last round, increase 1 stitch in the center of the sole for a total of 49 (55, 61) stitches.

Work in pattern across the stitches on needle 1.

TURN THE HEEL

You will now work back and forth on the stitches on needle 2 and will not work the stitches on needle 1 while turning the heel. Turn the heel as follows:

Row 1 (RS) K33 (37, 41), kf&b, k1, w&t.

Row 2 P20 (22, 24), pf&b, p1, w&t.

Row 3 K18 (20, 22), kf&b, k1, w&t.

LACY RIBS SOCKS (CONTINUED)

Row 4 P16 (18, 20), pf&b, p1, w&t.
Row 5 K14 (16, 18), kf&b, k1, w&t.
Row 6 P12 (14, 16), pf&b, p1, w&t.
Row 7 K10 (12, 14), kf&b, k1, w&t.
Row 8 P8 (10, 12), pf&b, p1, w&t.
Needle 2 now holds 57 (63, 69) stitches, having just completed a wrong-side row. On the right side, knit to the end of needle 2, knitting each wrap together with the stitch it wraps. Work across the instep stitches on needle 1 in the lace pattern.

HEEL FLAP
Work back and forth on the heel stitches on needle 2:

Row 1 (RS) K42 (47, 52) (knitting each wrap together with the stitch it wraps), ssk, turn.
Row 2 Sl1, p27 (31, 35), p2tog, turn.
Row 3 *Sl1, k1; repeat from * 14 (16, 18) times, ssk, turn.
Repeat rows 2 and 3 until all of the side stitches have been worked, ending with row 2.
Needle 2 now holds 29 (33, 37) stitches. On the last row, decrease 1 stitch in the center of the row. Needle 2 now holds 28 (32, 36) stitches.
Begin working in the round again.

You will continue to work the lace chart on needle 1 and begin to work the lace chart across needle 2, making sure you are starting on the same chart row as for needle 1.

FINISHING
When your sock is 1" (2.5cm) short of the desired leg length, work in ribbing as follows: p1, k2, p2 to the last stitch, p1. When the ribbing measures 1" (2.5cm), bind off very loosely in rib.

LACY RIBS SOCKS

---

key

	K
•	P
/	K2TOG
\	SSK
O	YO

lace chart

DIAGONAL LACE SOCKS

DIAGONAL LACE SOCKS (CONTINUED)

THE COMBINATION OF A SIMPLE DIAGONAL LACE WITH SOME PURL STITCHES
FOR TEXTURE MAKES A GORGEOUS SOCK THAT REALLY DESERVES A NAME
MORE CREATIVE THAN DIAGONAL LACE. THIS PATTERN WILL LOOK GOOD IN A
YARN WITH SOME SUBTLE VARIEGATION OR IN A HEATHERED OR SOLID YARN.

SIZE: M (L), 8 (9)" (20.5 [23]cm)

GAUGE: 8 stitches and 12 rows = 1" (2.5cm) in stockinette stitch

NEEDLES: 2 US size 0 (2mm) circular needles (or 1 long circular needle), or size needed to obtain gauge

YARN USED: 1 skein Dream in Color Smooshy Sock Yarn, 100% superfine Australian superwash merino, 4 oz (113.5g), 450 yd (411.5m), Strange Harvest ⓵ Superfine

---

Note: The pattern repeat for this chart is 12 rows. Note that only odd-numbered rows are shown on the chart; even-numbered rows are all plain knit.

TOE
Using a Turkish Cast-On, Figure-Eight Cast-On, or Judy's Magic Cast-On (page 20), cast on a total of 30 (34) stitches—15 (17) stitches on each needle. Knit across the stitches on each needle once. On the next round, increase 4 stitches as follows:
Needle 1 K1, M1, knit until the last stitch, M1, k1.
Needle 2 K1, M1, knit until the last stitch, M1, k1.
Then knit a round without increasing.
Repeat these 2 rounds until you have a total of 66 (74) stitches— 33 (37) stitches on each needle.

Note: If you prefer a pointier toe, you can cast on fewer stitches, but be sure to increase until you have 33 (37) stitches on each of the 2 needles.

Start the lace pattern:
Use the chart appropriate for the size of sock you are making.
Needle 1 (the instep stitches)
Work the chart 4 times, p1.
Needle 2 Knit across all of the stitches.
Continue in this manner, working as many repeats of the 5- (6-) row chart as necessary until approximately 3" (7.5cm) shy of the total length of the foot.

CREATE THE GUSSET
Round 1 Work across needle 1 in the lace pattern. Needle 2 (sole stitches): K1, M1, knit across to the last stitch, M1, k1.
Round 2 Work across needle 1 in the lace pattern. Needle 2 (sole stitches): Knit all stitches.
Repeat rounds 1 and 2 until you have 55 (61) stitches total on needle 2.
Work in pattern across the stitches on needle 1.

TURN THE HEEL
You will work back and forth on the stitches on needle 2 and will not knit the stitches on needle 1 while turning the heel. Turn the heel as follows:
Row 1 (RS) K37 (41), kf&b, k1, w&t.

Row 2 P22 (24), pf&b, p1, w&t.

Row 3 K20 (22), kf&b, k1, w&t.

Row 4 P18 (20), pf&b, p1, w&t.

Row 5 K16 (18), kf&b, k1, w&t.

Row 6 P14 (16), pf&b, p1, w&t.

Row 7 K12 (14), kf&b, k1, w&t.

Row 8 P10 (12), pf&b, p1, w&t.

The needle now holds 63 (69) stitches, having just ended a wrong-side row. On the right side, knit to the end of the needle, knitting each wrap together with the stitch it wraps. Work across the instep stitches on needles 1 and 2 in pattern.

HEEL FLAP

Work back and forth on the heel stitches:

Row 1 (RS) K47 (52) (knitting each wrap together with the stitch it wraps), ssk, turn.

Row 2 Sl1, p31 (35), p2tog, turn.

Row 3 *Sl1, k1; repeat from * 16 (18) times, ssk, turn.

Repeat rows 2 and 3 until all of the side stitches have been worked and end having worked row 2. Needle 2 now holds 33 (37) stitches. Begin working in the round again. Work the stitches on needle 1 as established above. Work the lace pattern over needle 2 as you did on needle 1, ensuring that you are starting in the correct place on the chart so that it corresponds with the chart on needle 1.

FINISHING

When your sock is 1" (2.5cm) short of the desired leg length, work in k1, p1 ribbing for 1" (2.5cm). Bind off very loosely in rib.

DIAGONAL LACE SOCKS

key

	K
•	P
\	SSK
O	YO

lace chart large

\	O						•	11
	\	O					•	9
		\	O				•	7
			\	O			•	5
				\	O		•	3
					\	O	•	1

9   7   5   3   1

lace chart medium

\	O					•	9
	\	O				•	7
		\	O			•	5
			\	O		•	3
				\	O	•	1

7   5   3   1

TIC-TAC-TOE-UP SOCKS

THESE SOCKS ARE JUST SLIGHTLY MORE CHALLENGING THAN THE PREVIOUS THREE, BUT THEY ARE STILL VERY EASY. AFTER YOU KNIT A FEW ROUNDS, YOU WILL GET THE HANG OF THE PATTERN. MAKE A PAIR FOR YOUR FAVORITE TIC-TAC-TOE AFICIONADO OR XBOX GAMER!

SIZE: M (L), 8¼ (9¼)" (21 [23.5]cm)

GAUGE: 8 stitches and 12 rows = 1" (2.5cm) in stockinette stitch

NEEDLES: 2 US size 0 (2mm) circular needles (or 1 long circular needle), or size needed to obtain gauge

YARN USED: 1½ skeins Colinette Jitterbug, 100% merino wool, 4 oz (113.5g), 317 yd (290m), Velvet Leaf **1** Superfine

Note: You may be able to get a pair of socks out of 1 skein of the yarn used if you are making smaller-than-average socks.

Note: The pattern repeat for this chart is 24 rows. Note that only odd-numbered rows are shown on the chart; even-numbered rows are all plain knit.

TOE

Using a Turkish Cast-On, Figure-Eight Cast-On, or Judy's Magic Cast-On (page 20), cast on a total of 30 (34) stitches—15 (17) stitches on each needle. Knit across the stitches on each needle once.

On the next round, increase 4 stitches as follows:

Needle 1 K1, M1, knit until the last stitch, M1, k1.

Needle 2 K1, M1, knit until the last stitch, M1, k1.

Then knit a round without increasing.

Repeat these 2 rounds until you have a total of 66 (74) stitches—33 (37) stitches on each needle.

Note: If you prefer a pointier toe, you can cast on fewer stitches, but be sure to increase until you have 33 (37) stitches on each of the 2 needles.

Start the lace pattern:

You will work the chart over needle 1 only (the instep stitches) and knit across needle 2.

Row 1 On needle 1, k1, work row 1 of the lace chart. Knit across the stitches on needle 2.

Row 2 (and all even-numbered rows) Knit across the stitches on needle 1 and needle 2.

Continue in this manner, working as many repeats of the 24-row chart as necessary until approximately 3" (7.5cm) shy of the total length of the foot.

CREATE THE GUSSET

Round 1 Work across needle 1 in the lace pattern. Needle 2 (sole stitches): K1, M1, knit across to the last stitch, M1, k1.

Round 2 Work across needle 1 in the lace pattern. Needle 2 (sole stitches): Knit all stitches.

Repeat rounds 1 and 2 until you have 55 (61) stitches total on needle 2.

Work in pattern across the stitches on needle 1.

TURN THE HEEL

You will now work back and forth on the stitches on needle 2 and will not knit the stitches on needle 1 while turning the heel. Turn the heel as follows:

Row 1 (RS) K37 (41), kf&b, k1, w&t.

Row 2 P22 (24), pf&b, p1, w&t.

Row 3 K20 (22), kf&b, k1, w&t.

Row 4 P18 (20), pf&b, p1, w&t.

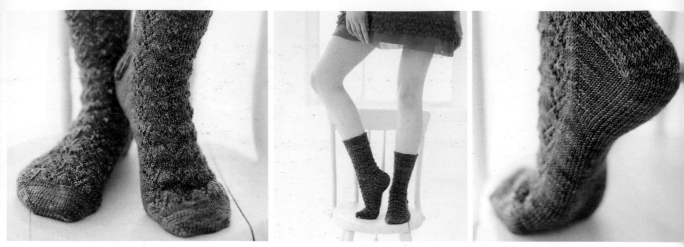

TICK-TAC-TOE-UP SOCKS (CONTINUED)

Row 5 K16 (18), kf&b, k1, w&t.
Row 6 P14 (16), pf&b, p1, w&t.
Row 7 K12 (14), kf&b, k1, w&t.
Row 8 P10 (12), pf&b, p1, w&t.
Needle 2 now holds 63 (69) stitches, having just completed a wrong-side row. On the right side, knit to the end of needle 2, knitting each wrap together with the stitch it wraps. Work across the instep stitches on needle 1 in the lace pattern.

HEEL FLAP

Work back and forth on the heel stitches:
Row 1 (RS) K47 (52) (knitting each wrap together with the stitch it wraps), ssk, turn.
Row 2 Sl1, p31 (35), p2tog, turn.
Row 3 *Sl1, k1; repeat from * 16 (18) times, ssk, turn.
Repeat rows 2 and 3 until all of the side stitches have been worked, and end having worked row 2. Needle 2 now holds 33 (37) stitches.

Begin working in the round again. You will continue to work the lace chart on needle 1. On needle 2, begin to work the lace chart as for needle 1, ensuring that you are on the same row as worked on needle 1.

FINISHING

When your sock is 1" (2.5cm) short of the desired leg length, work in k1, p1 ribbing for 1" (2.5cm). Bind off very loosely in rib.

TIC-TAC-TOE-UP SOCKS

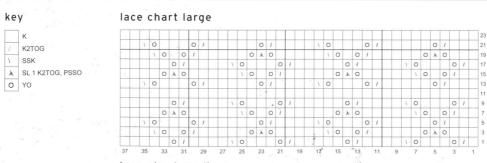

key

	K
/	K2TOG
\	SSK
λ	SL 1 K2TOG, PSSO
O	YO

lace chart large

lace chart medium

BUTTERFLY SOCKS

BUTTERFLY SOCKS (CONTINUED)

THIS DAINTY PATTERN REMINDS ME OF BUTTERFLIES—HENCE THE NAME. THERE'S A BIT OF EXCITEMENT IN THE PATTERN BECAUSE YOU ARE MAKING DOUBLE YARN OVERS, BUT THIS IS QUITE SIMPLE TO DO AND IT CREATES A LOVELY OPEN LACY EFFECT.

SIZE: M (L), 8 (9)" (20.5 [23]cm)

GAUGE: 8 stitches and 12 rows = 1" (2.5cm) in stockinette stitch

NEEDLES: 2 US size 0 (2mm) circular needles (or 1 long circular needle), or size needed to obtain gauge

YARN USED: 1 skein Cherry Tree Hill Supersock Solids, 100% luxury merino fingering weight, 4 oz (113.5g), 420 yd (384m), Pink (1) Superfine

---

TIP: KEEPING TRACK IN LACE CHARTS

When I'm knitting anything other than the easiest patterns, I find it useful to photocopy the chart and put it on a metal board with magnetic strips. You use one of the strips to mark your row in the pattern and move it up as you complete each round. These magnetic boards are available in many craft and knitting shops.

TOE

Using a Turkish Cast-On, Figure-Eight Cast-On, or Judy's Magic Cast-On (page 20), cast on a total of 32 (36) stitches—16 (18) stitches on each needle. Knit across the stitches on each needle once. On the next round, increase 4 stitches as follows:

Needle 1 K1, M1, knit until the last stitch, M1, k1.

Needle 2 K1, M1, knit until the last stitch, M1, k1.

Then knit a round without increasing.

Repeat these 2 rounds until you have a total of 64 (72) stitches—32 (36) stitches on each needle.

Note: If you prefer a pointier toe, you can cast on fewer stitches, but be sure to increase until you have 32 (36) stitches on each of the 2 needles.

Start the lace pattern:
Needle 1 holds the instep stitches and Needle 2 holds the sole stitches.

Row 1 On needle 1, k1 (3), work the 10 stitches of row 1 of the lace pattern 3 times, k1 (3). Knit across needle 2.

Row 2 On needle 1, k1 (3), work the 10 stitches of row 2 of the lace pattern 3 times, k1 (3). Knit across needle 2.

Continue in this manner until you have worked 8 rows of the pattern and have completed 1 repeat of the chart.

Row 9 On needle 1, k6 (8), work the 10 stitches of row 1 of the lace pattern 2 times, k6 (8). Knit across needle 2.

Row 10 On needle 1, k6 (8), work the 10 stitches of row 2 of the lace pattern 2 times, k6 (8). Knit across needle 2.

Continue in this manner until you have worked a total of 16 rows; then start again from row 1. Continue in this manner, working as many repeats of the chart as necessary until approximately 3" (7.5cm) shy of the total length of the foot.

CREATE THE GUSSET

Round 1 Work across needle 1 in the lace pattern. Needle 2 (sole stitches): K1, M1, knit across to the last stitch, M1, k1.

Round 2 Work across needle 1 in the lace pattern. Needle 2 (sole stitches): Knit all stitches.

Repeat rounds 1 and 2 until you have 54 (60) stitches total on needle 2. On the last round, increase 1 stitch in the center of the sole for a total of 55 (61) stitches.

Work in pattern across the stitches on needle 1.

TURN THE HEEL

You will now work back and forth on the stitches on needle 2 and will not knit the stitches on needle 1 while turning the heel. Turn the heel as follows:

Row 1 (RS) K37 (41), kf&b, k1, w&t.
Row 2 P22 (24), pf&b, p1, w&t.
Row 3 K20 (22), kf&b, k1, w&t.
Row 4 P18 (20), pf&b, p1, w&t.
Row 5 K16 (18), kf&b, k1, w&t.
Row 6 P14 (16), pf&b, p1, w&t.
Row 7 K12 (14), kf&b, K1, w&t.
Row 8 P10 (12), pf&b, P1, w&t.
Needle 2 now holds 63 (69) stitches, having just completed a wrong-side row. On the right side, knit to the end of needle 2, knitting each wrap together with the stitch it wraps. Work across the instep stitches on needle 1 in the lace pattern.

HEEL FLAP

Work back and forth on the heel stitches:
Row 1 (RS) K47 (52) (knitting each wrap together with the stitch it wraps), ssk, turn.

Row 2 Sl1, p31 (35), p2tog, turn.
Row 3 *Sl1, k1; repeat from * 16 (18) times, ssk, turn.
Repeat rows 2 and 3 until all side stitches have been worked, ending with row 2. Needle 2 now holds 33 (37) stitches. On the last row, decrease 1 stitch in the center of the row. The needle now holds 32 (36) stitches.
Begin working in the round again. Make sure that you are starting in the right place on the chart so that it corresponds with the chart on needle 1, and start working the lace pattern on needle 2.

FINISHING

When your sock is 1" (2.5cm) short of the desired leg length, work in k2, p2 ribbing for 1" (2.5cm). Bind off very loosely in rib.

BUTTERFLY SOCKS

key

☐	K
•	P
/	K2TOG
\	SSK
O	YO

lace chart

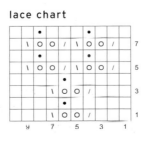
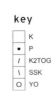

ON-HOLD SOCKS

ON-HOLD SOCKS (CONTINUED)

THESE SOCKS GOT THEIR NAME BECAUSE I WAS ON THE TELEPHONE, ON HOLD, AND BORED. FORTUNATELY, THERE WAS A PENCIL AND A BIT OF GRAPH PAPER NEARBY, SO I CHARTED UP A PRETTY SCROLLWORK DESIGN WHILE LISTENING TO THE MUZAK.

SIZE: M (L), 8¼ (9¼)" (21 [23.5]cm)

GAUGE: 8 stitches and 12 rows = 1" (2.5cm) in stockinette stitch

NEEDLES: 2 US size 0 (2mm) circular needles (or 1 long circular needle), or size needed to obtain gauge

YARN USED: 2 skeins Shibui Knits Sock, 100% superwash merino wool, 1¾ oz (50g), 191 yd (174.5m), Sky (color number 3115) **(1)** Superfine

---

Note: The pattern repeat for this chart is 12 rows. Note that only odd-numbered rows are shown on the chart; even-numbered rows are all plain knit.

TOE
Using a Turkish Cast-On, Figure-Eight Cast-On, or Judy's Magic Cast-On (page 20), cast on a total of 30 (34) stitches—15 (17) stitches on each needle. Knit across the stitches on each needle once. On the next round, increase 4 stitches as follows:
Needle 1 K1, M1, knit until the last stitch, M1, k1.
Needle 2 K1, M1, knit until the last stitch, M1, k1.
Then knit a round without increasing.

Repeat these 2 rounds until you have a total of 66 (74) stitches—33 (37) stitches on each needle.

Note: If you prefer a pointier toe, you can cast on fewer stitches, but be sure to increase until you have 33 (37) stitches on each of the 2 needles.

Start the lace pattern:
You will work the chart over needle 1 only (the instep stitches) and knit across the stitches on needle 2.
Row 1 On needle 1, k0 (2), work row 1 of the lace chart over the next 33 stitches, k0 (2). Knit across the stitches on needle 2.
Row 2 (and all even-numbered rows) Knit across the stitches on needle 1 and needle 2.

Continue in this manner, working as many repeats of the 12-row chart as necessary until approximately 3" (7.5cm) shy of the total length of the foot.

CREATE THE GUSSET
Round 1 Work across needle 1 in the lace pattern. Needle 2 (sole stitches): K1, M1, knit across to the last stitch, M1, k1.
Round 2 Work across needle 1 in the lace pattern. Needle 2 (sole stitches): Knit all stitches.
Repeat rounds 1 and 2 until you have 55 (61) stitches total on needle 2.
Work in pattern across the stitches on needle 1.

TURN THE HEEL

You will now work back and forth on the stitches on needle 2 and will not knit the stitches on needle 1 while turning the heel. Turn the heel as follows:

Row 1 (RS) K37 (41), kf&B, k1, w&t.
Row 2 P22 (24), pf&b, p1, w&t.
Row 3 K20 (22), kf&b, k1, w&t.
Row 4 P18 (20), pf&b, p1, w&t.
Row 5 K16 (18), kf&b, k1, w&t.
Row 6 P14 (16), pf&b, p1, w&t.
Row 7 K12 (14), kf&b, k1, w&t
Row 8 P10 (12), pf&b, p1, w&t.
Needle 2 now holds 63 (69) stitches, having just completed a wrong-side row. On the right side, knit to the end of needle 2, knitting each wrap together with the stitch it wraps. Work across the instep stitches on needle 1 in the lace pattern.

HEEL FLAP

Work back and forth on the heel stitches:

Row 1 (RS) K47 (52) (knitting each wrap together with the stitch it wraps), ssk, turn.
Row 2 Sl1, p31 (35), p2tog, turn.
Row 3 *Sl1, k1; repeat from * 16 (18) times, ssk, turn.
Repeat rows 2 and 3 until all of the side stitches have been worked, ending with row 2. Needle 2 now holds 33 (37) stitches.
Begin working in the round again. You will continue to work the lace chart on needle 1. On needle 2, work as follows, ensuring you are on the same row as worked on needle 1:
k0 (2), work the first 3 stitches of the lace chart, k27, work the last 3 stitches of the lace chart, k0 (2).

FINISHING

When your sock is 1" (2.5cm) short of the desired leg length, work in ribbing as follows:
On needle 1: P0 (2), work the first 3 stitches of the lace chart (p3, k3) 4 times, p3, work the last 3 stitches of the lace chart, p0 (2). Repeat for needle 2. Work this ribbing for 1" (2.5cm). Bind off very loosely in rib.

ON-HOLD SOCKS

key

	K
/	K2TOG
\	SSK
λ	SL 1 K2TOG, PSSO
O	YO

lace chart

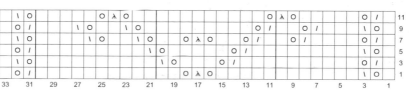

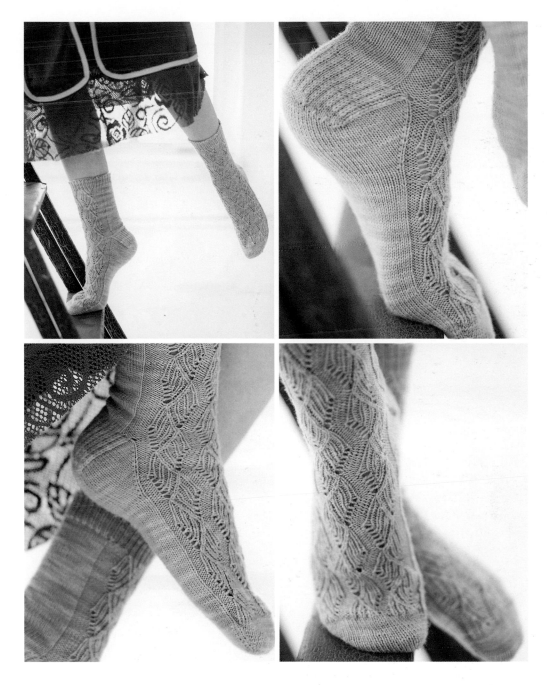

RIBBED RIBBONS SOCKS

RIBBED RIBBONS SOCKS (CONTINUED)

THESE SOCKS INCORPORATE A BIT OF TEXTURE WITH LACE. THE RIBBONS ARE RIBBED AND SWIRL GENTLY AROUND THE FRONT OF THE SOCK. THERE IS SOME STRETCH TO THE RIBBING, MAKING THE SOCKS CONFORM WELL TO DIFFERENT SIZES, SO THEY FIT BEAUTIFULLY.

SIZE: M (L), 8¼ (9¼)" (21 [23.5]cm)

GAUGE: 8 stitches and 12 rows = 1" (2.5cm) in stockinette stitch

NEEDLES: 2 US size 0 (2mm) circular needles (or 1 long circular needle), or size needed to obtain gauge

YARN USED: 1 skein Dream in Color Smooshy Sock Yarn, 100% superfine Australian superwash merino, 4 oz (113.5g), 450 yd (411.5m), Giant Peach (1) Superfine

---

TOE
Using a Turkish Cast-On, Figure-Eight Cast-On, or Judy's Magic Cast-On (page 20), cast on a total of 30 (34) stitches—15 (17) stitches on each needle. Knit across the stitches on each needle once. On the next round, increase 4 stitches as follows:
Needle 1 K1, M1, knit until the last stitch, M1, k1.
Needle 2 K1, M1, knit until the last stitch, M1, k1.
Then knit a round without increasing.
Repeat these 2 rounds until you have a total of 66 (74) stitches—33 (37) stitches on each needle.

Note: If you prefer a pointier toe, you can cast on fewer stitches, but be sure to increase until you have 33 (37) stitches on each of the 2 needles.

Start the lace pattern:
You will work the chart over needle 1 only (the instep stitches) and knit the stitches across needle 2.
On needle 1, p0 (2), work the 10 stitches of the chart pattern 3 times, then work the first 3 stitches of the chart again, p0 (2). Knit across the stitches on needle 2.
Continue in this manner, working as many repeats of the 24-row chart as necessary until approximately 3" (7.5cm) shy of the total length of the foot.

CREATE THE GUSSET
Round 1 Work across needle 1 in the lace pattern. Needle 2 (sole stitches): K1, M1, knit across to the last stitch, M1, k1.
Round 2 Work across needle 1 in the lace pattern. Needle 2 (sole stitches): Knit all stitches.
Repeat rounds 1 and 2 until you have 55 (61) stitches total on needle 2.
Work in pattern across the stitches on needle 1.

TURN THE HEEL
You will now work back and forth on the stitches on needle 2 and will not knit the stitches on needle 1 while turning the heel. Turn the heel as follows:
Row 1 (RS) K37 (41), kf&b, k1, w&t.

Row 2 P22 (24), pf&b, p1, w&t.
Row 3 K20 (22), kf&b, k1, w&t.
Row 4 P18 (20), pf&b, p1, w&t.
Row 5 K16 (18), kf&b, k1, w&t.
Row 6 P14 (16), pf&b, p1, w&t.
Row 7 K12 (14), kf&b, k1, w&t.
Row 8 P10 (12), pf&b, p1, w&t.
Needle 2 now holds 63 (69) stitches, having just completed a wrong-side row. On the right side, knit to the end of needle 2, knitting each wrap together with the stitch it wraps. Work across the instep stitches on needle 1 in the lace pattern.

HEEL FLAP

Work back and forth on the heel stitches:

Row 1 (RS) K47 (52) (knitting each wrap together with the stitch it wraps), ssk, turn.
Row 2 Sl1, p31 (35), p2tog, turn.
Row 3 [Sl1, k1] 16 (18) times, ssk, turn.

Repeat rows 2 and 3 until all of the side stitches have been worked, and end having worked row 2. Needle 2 now holds 33 (37) stitches.

Begin working in the round again.

You will continue to work the lace chart on needle 1. On needle 2, work as follows: p3 (5), k27, p3 (5).

FINISHING

When your sock is 1" (2.5cm) short of the desired leg length, work in k1, p1 ribbing. Work the ribbing for 1" (2.5cm). Bind off very loosely in rib.

RIBBED RIBBONS SOCKS

key

☐	K
•	P
/	K2TOG
\	SSK
O	YO

lace chart

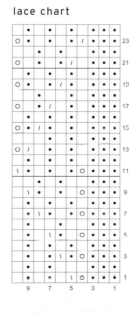

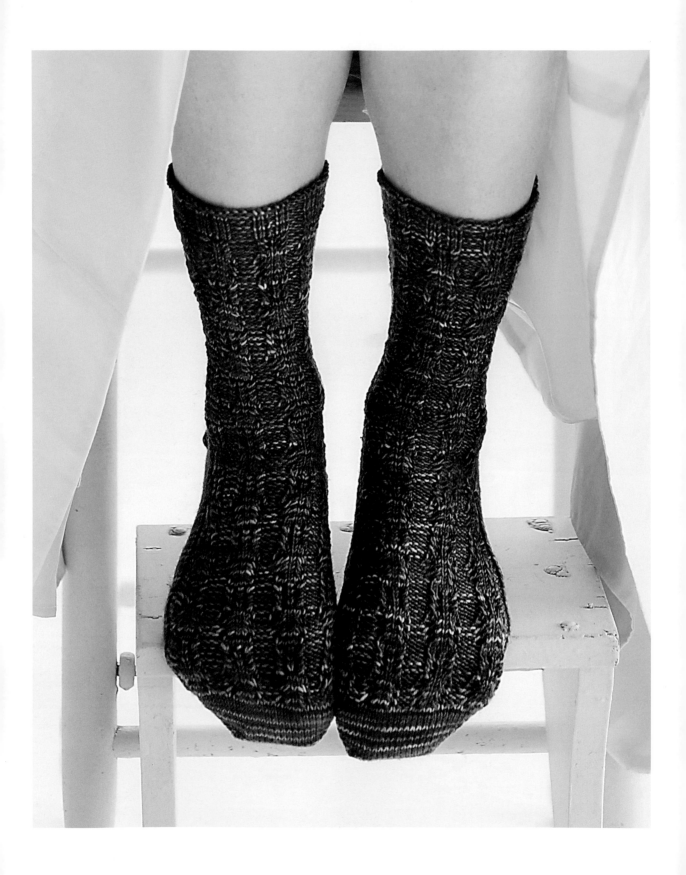

TRILOBITE SOCKS

TRILOBITE SOCKS (CONTINUED)

WHILE I WAS BRAINSTORMING IDEAS FOR SOCKS, I KNIT A SWATCH OF THIS LACE PATTERN. AS THE PATTERN EMERGED, I THOUGHT "TRILOBITES! THEY LOOK LIKE TRILOBITES!" BECAUSE I'VE HAD A FONDNESS FOR TRILOBITES THAT DATES BACK TO CHILDHOOD, WHEN MY BROTHER AND I CREATED DOZENS OF PLASTIC TRILOBYTES WITH A "THINGMAKER" TOY, I KNEW I HAD TO CREATE A DESIGN USING THIS PATTERN. A SOCK WAS BORN.

SIZE: M (L), 8 (9)" (20.5 [23]cm)

GAUGE: 8 stitches and 12 rows = 1" (2.5cm) in stockinette stitch

NEEDLES: 2 US size 0 (2mm) circular needles (or 1 long circular needle), or size needed to obtain gauge

YARN USED: 1 skein Socks That Rock Lightweight, 100% superwash merino wool, 4½ oz (127.5g), 360 yd (329m), Tanzanite **①** Superfine

---

TOE

Using a Turkish Cast-On, Figure-Eight Cast-On, or Judy's Magic Cast-On (page 20), cast on a total of 30 (34) stitches—15 (17) stitches on each needle. Knit across the stitches on each needle once. On the next round, increase 4 stitches as follows:

Needle 1 K1, M1, knit until the last stitch, M1, k1.

Needle 2 K1, M1, knit until the last stitch, M1, k1.

Then knit a round without increasing.

Repeat these 2 rounds until you have a total of 66 (74) stitches—33 (37) stitches on each needle.

Note: If you prefer a pointier toe, you can cast on fewer stitches, but be sure to increase until you have 33 (37) stitches on each of the 2 needles.

Start the lace pattern:

You will work the chart over needle 1 only (the instep stitches) and will knit across the stitches on needle 2.

Row 1 On needle 1, work stitches 1–8 (1–9) of row 1 of the chart 4 times, then work stitch 9 (10). Knit across the stitches on needle 2.

Row 2 On needle 1, work stitches 1–8 (1–9) of row 2 of the chart 4 times, then work stitch 9 (10). Knit across the stitches on needle 2.

Continue in this manner, working as many repeats of the chart as necessary until approximately 3" (7.5cm) shy of the total length of the foot.

CREATE THE GUSSET

Round 1 Work across needle 1 in pattern. Needle 2 (sole stitches): K1, M1, knit across to the last stitch, M1, k1.

Round 2 Work across needle 1 in pattern. Needle 2 (sole stitches): Knit all stitches.

Repeat rounds 1 and 2 until you have 55 (61) stitches total on needle 2.

Work in pattern across the stitches on needle 1.

TURN THE HEEL

You will now work back and forth on the stitches on needle 2 and will not work the stitches on needle 1 while turning the heel. Turn the heel as follows:

Row 1 (RS) K37 (41), kf&b, k1, w&t.

Row 2 P22 (24), pf&b, p1, w&t.
Row 3 K20 (22), kf&b, k1, w&t.
Row 4 P18 (20), pf&b, p1, w&t.
Row 5 K16 (18), kf&b, k1, w&t.
Row 6 P14 (16), pf&b, p1, w&t.
Row 7 K12 (14), kf&b, k1, w&t.
Row 8 P10 (12), pf&b, p1, w&t.
Needle 2 now holds 63 (69) stitches, having just completed a wrong-side row. On the right side, knit to the end of needle 2, knitting each wrap together with the stitch it wraps. Work across the instep stitches on needle 1 in pattern.

HEEL FLAP

Work back and forth on the heel stitches on needle 2:

Row 1 (RS) K47 (52) (knitting each wrap together with the stitch it wraps), ssk, turn.
Row 2 Sl1, p31 (35), p2tog, turn.
Row 3 [sl1, k1] 16 (18) times, ssk, turn.
Repeat rows 2 and 3 until all of the side stitches have been worked, and end having worked row 2. Needle 2 now holds 33 (37) stitches.
Begin working in the round again. Making sure that you are starting in the correct place on the chart so that it corresponds with the chart on needle 1, work across needle 2 in the same manner as described for needle 1.

FINISHING

When you are 1" (2.5cm) short of the desired length of the sock, begin the ribbing:

Size M:

Needle 1 K1, p1, (k2, p1, k2, p3) 3 times, k2, p1, k2, p1, k1.
Needle 2 As for needle 1.

Size L:

Needle 1 K1, p2, (k2, p1, k2, p1, k2, p1) 3 times, k2, p1, k2, p1, k1.
Needle 2 As for needle 1.
Work this ribbing for 1" (2.5cm).

TRILOBITE SOCKS

key

	K
•	P
/	K2TOG
\	SSK
O	YO

lace chart large

lace chart medium

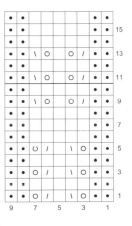

HEARTS AND FLOWERS SOCKS

HEARTS AND FLOWERS SOCKS (CONTINUED)

THESE ARE "PATCHWORK" SOCKS, DIVIDED INTO SQUARES WITH ALTERNATING MOTIFS OF HEARTS AND FLOWERS. IF YOU ARE FEELING AMBITIOUS, YOU COULD USE THIS PATTERN AS A STARTING POINT FOR CREATING YOUR OWN PATCHWORK DESIGN. INSTEAD OF HEARTS AND FLOWERS, INSERT DIFFERENT MOTIFS IN EACH SQUARE—FOR EXAMPLE, ALPHABET LETTERS OR NUMBERS.

SIZE: M (L), 8½ (9½)" (21.5 [24]cm)

GAUGE: 8 stitches and 12 rows = 1" (2.5cm) in stockinette stitch

NEEDLES: 2 US size 0 (2mm) circular needles (or 1 long circular needle), or size needed to obtain gauge

YARN USED: 2 skeins Claudia Hand Painted Yarns Fingering, 100% merino wool, 1¾ oz (50g), 172 yd (157m), Marigold ⑪ Superfine

TOE

Using a Turkish Cast-On, Figure-Eight Cast-On, or Judy's Magic Cast-On (page 20), cast on a total of 30 (34) stitches—15 (17) stitches on each needle. Knit across the stitches on each needle once. On the next round, increase 4 stitches as follows:

Needle 1 K1, M1, knit until the last stitch, M1, k1.

Needle 2 K1, M1, knit until the last stitch, M1, k1.

Then knit a round without increasing.

Repeat these 2 rounds until you have a total of 66 (74) stitches—33 (37) stitches on each needle.

Note: If you prefer a pointier toe, you can cast on fewer stitches, but be sure to increase until you have 33 (37) stitches on each of the 2 needles.

Start the lace chart pattern:

You will work the chart over needle 1 only (the instep stitches) and will knit the stitches across needle 2.

Row 1 On needle 1, k0 (2), work the 33 stitches of row 1 of chart 1, k0 (2). Needle 2: Knit across all 33 (37) stitches.

Row 2 On needle 1, k0 (2), work the 33 stitches of row 2 of chart 1, k0 (2). Needle 2: Knit across all 33 (37) stitches.

Continue in this manner, working the 20 rows of chart 1. When you have completed chart 1, start chart 2 in the same manner.

Note: For the remainder of the sock, you will alternate using chart 1 and chart 2.

Work until approximately 3" (7.5cm) shy of the total length of the foot.

CREATE THE GUSSET

Round 1 Work across needle 1 in the chart pattern. Needle 2 (sole stitches): K1, M1, knit across to the last stitch, M1, k1.

Round 2 Work across needle 1 in the chart pattern. Needle 2 (sole stitches): Knit all stitches.

Repeat rounds 1 and 2 until you have 55 (61) stitches total on needle 2.

Work in pattern across the stitches on needle 1.

TURN THE HEEL

You will now work back and forth on the stitches on needle 2 and will not work the stitches on needle 1 while turning the heel. Turn the heel as follows:

Row 1 (RS) K37 (41), kf&b, k1, w&t.

Row 2 P22 (24), pf&b, p1, w&t.

Row 3 K20 (22), kf&b, k1, w&t.

Row 4 P18 (20), pf&b, p1, w&t.
Row 5 K16 (18), kf&b, k1, w&t.
Row 6 P14 (16), pf&b, p1, w&t.
Row 7 K12 (14), kf&b, k1, w&t.
Row 8 P10 (12), pf&b, p1, w&t.
Needle 2 now holds 63 (69) stitches, having just completed a wrong-side row. On the right side, knit to the end of needle 2, knitting each wrap together with the stitch it wraps. Work across the instep stitches on needle 1 in the chart pattern.

HEEL FLAP

Work back and forth on the heel stitches on needle 2:
Row 1 (RS) K47 (52) (knitting each wrap together with the stitch it wraps), ssk, turn.
Row 2 Sl1, p31 (35), p2tog, turn.
Row 3 *Sl1, k1; repeat from * 16 (18) times, ssk, turn.
Repeat rows 2 and 3 until all of the side stitches have been worked, and end having worked Row 2. Needle 2 now holds 33 (37) stitches.
Begin working in the round again. Continue working the charts on needle 1 as set, and knit the stitches across needle 2. Continue in this manner until the leg of the sock is the desired length; then work a picot edge.

FINISHING
Picot Edge
Next round K2tog, yo around all 66 (74) stitches.
Knit 6 rounds to form a hem, and bind off very loosely. Leave a yarn tail of about 15" (38cm). Fold this hem to the inside of the sock (it will fold naturally along the round with the yarn overs), and loosely sew it to the inside of the sock, using a tapestry needle and the yarn tail.

HEARTS AND FLOWERS SOCKS

key

lace chart 1
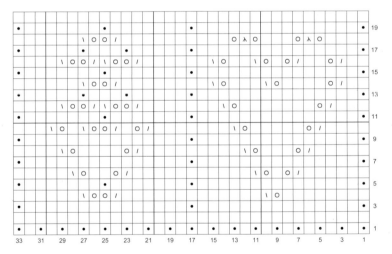

lace chart 2
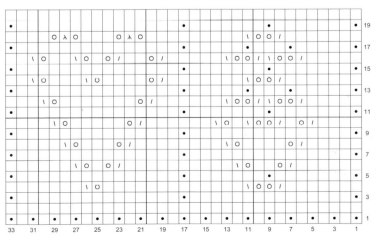

LACE AND CABLE SOCKS

LACE AND CABLE SOCKS (CONTINUED)

I'VE SNEAKED A BIT OF CABLE WORK INTO THIS LACE SOCK. THE SMALL CABLES CONTRAST NICELY WITH THE LACY LATTICE MOTIF. BECAUSE THE LACE MOTIF IS LARGE AND SOMEWHAT OPEN, YOU CAN USE A HEATHERED OR SLIGHTLY VARIEGATED YARN WITHOUT WORRYING ABOUT IT OBSCURING THE PATTERN.

SIZE: S (M, L), 7¼ (8¼, 9¼)" (18.5 [21, 23.5]cm)

GAUGE: 8 stitches and 12 rows = 1" (2.5cm) in stockinette stitch

NEEDLES: 2 US size 0 (2mm) circular needles (or 1 long circular needle), or size needed to obtain gauge

YARN USED: 1 skein Dream in Color Smooshy Sock Yarn, 100% superfine Australian superwash merino wool, 4 oz (113.5g), 450 yd (411.5m), Chinatown Apple ⓘ Superfine

---

TOE

Using a Turkish Cast-On, Figure-Eight Cast-On, or Judy's Magic Cast-On (page 20), cast on a total of 26 (30, 34) stitches—13 (15, 17) stitches on each needle. Knit across the stitches on each needle once. On the next round, increase 4 stitches as follows:

Needle 1 K1, M1, knit until the last stitch, M1, k1.

Needle 2 K1, M1, knit until the last stitch, M1, k1.

Then knit a round without increasing.

Repeat these 2 rounds until you have a total of 58 (66, 74) stitches—29 (33, 37) stitches on each needle.

Note: If you prefer a pointier toe, you can cast on fewer stitches, but be sure to increase until you have 29 (33, 37) stitches on each of the 2 needles.

Start the lace pattern:

You will work the chart over needle 1 only (the instep stitches) and will knit across the stitches on needle 2.

Row 1 On needle 1, work row 1 of the left cable chart, place marker, k1 (3, 5), place marker, work row 1 of the lace chart over the next 17 stitches, place marker, k1 (3, 5), place marker, work row 1 of the right cable chart. Needle 2: Knit across the stitches.

Row 2 On needle 1, work row 2 of the left cable chart, place marker, k1 (3, 5), place marker, work row 2 of the lace chart over the next 17 stitches, place marker, k1 (3, 5), place marker, work row 2 of the right cable chart. Knit across the stitches on needle 2.

Continue in this manner, working as many rows as necessary until approximately 3" (7.5cm) shy of the total length of the foot.

CREATE THE GUSSET

Round 1 Work across needle 1 in the chart patterns. Needle 2 (sole stitches): K1, M1, knit across to the last stitch, M1, k1.

Round 2 Work across needle 1 in the chart pattern. Needle 2 (sole stitches): Knit all stitches.

Repeat rounds 1 and 2 until you have 49 (55, 61) stitches total on needle 2.

Work in pattern across the stitches on needle 1.

TURN THE HEEL

You will now work back and forth on the stitches on needle 2 and

will not work the stitches on needle 1 while turning the heel. Turn the heel as follows:

Row 1 (RS) K33 (37, 41), kf&b, k1, w&t.

Row 2 P20 (22, 24), pf&b, p1, w&t.

Row 3 K18 (20, 22), kf&b, k1, w&t.

Row 4 P16 (18, 20), pf&b, p1, w&t.

Row 5 K14 (16, 18), kf&b, k1, w&t.

Row 6 P12 (14, 16), pf&b, p1, w&t.

Row 7 K10 (12, 14), kf&b, k1, w&t.

Row 8 P8 (10, 12), pf&b, p1, w&t.

Needle 2 now holds 57 (63, 69) stitches, having just completed a wrong-side row. On the right side, knit to the end of needle 2, knitting each wrap together with the stitch it wraps. Work across the instep stitches on needle 1 in the lace pattern.

HEEL FLAP

Work back and forth on the heel stitches on needle 2:

Row 1 (RS) K42 (47, 52) (knitting each wrap together with the stitch it wraps), ssk, turn.

Row 2 Sl1, p27 (31, 35), p2tog, turn.

Row 3 *Sl1, k1; repeat from * 14 (16, 18) times, ssk, turn.

Repeat rows 2 and 3 until all of the side stitches have been worked, and end having worked row 2. Needle 2 now holds 29 (33, 37) stitches.

Begin working in the round again. You will continue to work the charts as set on needle 1.

On needle 2, work the left cable chart, place marker, k19 (23, 27), place marker, work the right cable chart. (**Note:** Make sure that where you start work on the cable charts on needle 2 corresponds to the correct row of the cable charts you are working on needle 1.)

FINISHING

When your sock is 1" (2.5cm) short of the desired leg length, work in k1, p1 ribbing for 1" (2.5cm). Bind off very loosely in rib.

LACE AND CABLE SOCKS

key

☐	K
•	P
/	K2TOG
\	SSK
λ	SL 1 K2TOG, PSSO
O	YO
⋁	SL1 as to P
	SL1 to CN, hold at front, K2, K1 from CN
	Slip first 2 sts to CN, hold at back, K next st, then k 2 sts from CN

lace chart

(rows numbered: 15, 13, 11, 9, 7, 5, 3, 1 — columns numbered: 17, 15, 13, 11, 9, 7, 5, 3, 1)

left cable chart

(rows 3, 1 — columns 5, 3, 1)

right cable chart

(rows 3, 1 — columns 5, 3, 1)

RIDING ON THE METRO SOCKS

RIDING ON THE METRO SOCKS (CONTINUED)

WHILE I WAS RIDING THE SUBWAY ONE DAY, A GIRL WEARING A MACHINE-KNIT LACY CARDIGAN GOT ON. FROM WHERE I WAS SITTING, I COULD BARELY MAKE OUT THE LACE PATTERN, BUT IT GAVE ME AN IDEA FOR A SOCK. I CHARTED MY INTERPRETATION OF THE PATTERN, AN ELEGANT LACE LOZENGE, AS SOON AS I ARRIVED AT MY DESTINATION.

SIZE: M (L), 8¼ (9¼)" (21 [23.5]cm)

GAUGE: 8 stitches and 12 rows = 1" (2.5cm) in stockinette stitch

NEEDLES: 2 US size 0 (2mm) circular needles (or 1 long circular needle), or size needed to obtain gauge

YARN USED: 2 skeins Lorna's Laces Shepherd Sock, 80% superwash wool and 20% nylon, 2 oz (56.5g), 215 yd (196.5m), Lavender (1) Superfine

---

Note: The pattern repeat for this chart is 24 rows. Note that only odd-numbered rows are shown on the chart; even-numbered rows are all plain knit.

TOE
Using a Turkish Cast-On, Figure-Eight Cast-On, or Judy's Magic Cast-On (page 20), cast on a total of 30 (34) stitches—15 (17) stitches on each needle. Knit across the stitches on each needle once. On the next round, increase 4 stitches as follows:
Needle 1 K1, M1, knit until the last stitch, M1, k1.
Needle 2 K1, M1, knit until the last stitch, M1, k1.
Then knit a round without increasing.

Repeat these 2 rounds until you have a total of 66 (74) stitches—33 (37) stitches on each needle.

Note: If you prefer a pointier toe, you can cast on fewer stitches, but be sure to increase until you have 33 (37) stitches on each of the 2 needles.

Start the lace pattern:
You will work the chart over needle 1 only (the instep stitches) and will knit across the stitches on needle 2.
Row 1 On needle 1, k0 (2), work row 1 of the lace chart over the next 33 stitches, k0 (2). Needle 2: Knit across all stitches.
Row 2 (and all even-numbered rows) Knit across all stitches on needle 1 and needle 2.
Continue in this manner, working as many repeats of the 24-row chart as necessary until approximately 3" (7.5cm) shy of the total length of the foot.

CREATE THE GUSSET
Round 1 Work across needle 1 in the lace pattern. Needle 2 (sole stitches): K1, M1, knit across to the last stitch, M1, k1.
Round 2 Work across needle 1 in the lace pattern. Needle 2 (sole stitches): Knit all stitches.
Repeat rounds 1 and 2 until you have 55 (61) stitches total on needle 2.
Work in pattern across the stitches on needle 1.

TURN THE HEEL

You will now work back and forth on the stitches on needle 2 and will not knit the stitches on needle 1 while turning the heel. Turn the heel as follows:

Row 1 (RS) K37 (41), kf&b, k1, w&t.
Row 2 P22 (24), pf&b, p1, w&t.
Row 3 K20 (22), kf&b, k1, w&t.
Row 4 P18 (20), pf&b, p1, w&t.
Row 5 K16 (18), kf&b, k1, w&t.
Row 6 P14 (16), pf&b, p1, w&t.
Row 7 K12 (14), kf&b, k1, w&t.
Row 8 P10 (12), pf&b, p1, w&t.
Needle 2 now holds 63 (69) stitches, having just completed a wrong-side row. On the right side, knit to the end of needle 2, knitting each wrap together with the stitch it wraps. Work across the instep stitches on needle 1 in the lace pattern.

HEEL FLAP

Work back and forth on the heel stitches:

Row 1 (RS) K47 (52) (knitting each wrap together with the stitch it wraps), ssk, turn.
Row 2 Sl1, p31 (35), p2tog, turn.
Row 3 [Sl1, k1] 16 (18) times, ssk, turn.
Repeat rows 2 and 3 until all side stitches have been worked, and end having worked row 2. Needle 2 now holds 33 (37) stitches.

Begin working in the round again. You will continue to work the lace chart on needle 1. On needle 2, work as follows:

On odd-numbered rows: K1 (3), (yo, sl1, k2tog, psso, yo), k11, (yo, sl1, k2tog, psso, yo), k11, (yo, sl1, k2tog, psso), yo, k1 (3).
On even-numbered rows: Knit across stitches.

FINISHING

When your sock is 1" (2.5cm) short of the desired leg length, work in k1, p1 ribbing for 1" (2.5cm). Bind off very loosely in rib.

RIDING ON THE METRO SOCKS

key

	K
/	K2TOG
\	SSK
λ	SL 1 K2TOG, PSSO
O	YO

lace chart

33	31	29	27	25	23	21	19	17	15	13	11	9	7	5	3	1	
O λ O	\ O		O \	O /	O λ O	\ O		O \	O /	O λ O	23
O λ O	/ O		O \	O λ O	/ O		O \	O λ O	21
O λ O	/ O		O \	O λ O	/ O		O \	O λ O	19
O λ O	\ O	/ O		O /	O λ O	\ O	/ O		O /	O λ O	17
O λ O	\ O	O λ O		O /	O λ O	\ O	O λ O	O /	O λ O	15
O λ O	\ O	O λ O		O /	O λ O	\ O	O λ O	O /	O λ O	13
O λ O	\ O	O λ O		O /	O λ O	\ O	O λ O	O /	O λ O	11
O λ O	\ O	/ O		O /	O λ O	\ O	/ O		O /	O λ O	9
O λ O	\ O		O /	O λ O	\ O		O /	O λ O	7
O λ O	\ O	O /	O λ O	\ O	O /	O λ O	5
O λ O		O /	O λ O		O /	O λ O	3
O λ O		O /	O λ O		O /	O λ O	1

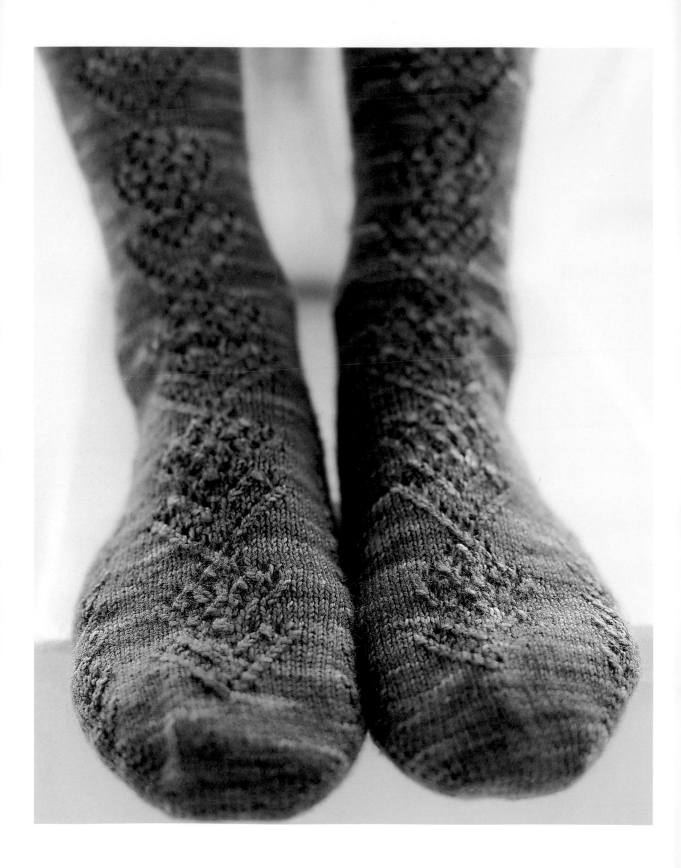

SHERI'S POSIES SOCKS

SHERI'S POSIES SOCKS (CONTINUED)

MY FRIEND SHERI LOVES MY TRILOBITE SOCKS (PAGE 68) BUT DOESN'T LIKE THE NAME BECAUSE SHE SAYS A TRILOBITE IS A BUG (AN EXTINCT BUG, BUT A BUG ALL THE SAME). SO I DESIGNED THIS SOCK, WITH A LARGE, PRETTY POSY MOTIF, JUST FOR HER—BUT YOU CAN MAKE THEM, TOO.

SIZE: M (L), 8¼ (9¼)" (21 [23.5]cm)

GAUGE: 8 stitches and 12 rows = 1" (2.5cm) in stockinette stitch

NEEDLES: 2 US size 0 (2mm) circular needles (or 1 long circular needle), or size needed to obtain gauge

YARN USED: 1 skein Fleece Artist Basic Merino 2/6 Sock, 100% machine washable merino wool, 4 oz (113.5g), 370 yd (338.5m), Teal **1** Superfine

---

Note: The pattern repeat for this chart is 32 rows. Note that only odd-numbered rows are shown on the chart; even-numbered rows are all plain knit.

TOE
Using a Turkish Cast-On, Figure-Eight Cast-On, or Judy's Magic Cast-On (page 20), cast on a total of 30 (34) stitches—15 (17) stitches on each needle. Knit across the stitches on each needle once.
On the next round, increase 4 stitches as follows:
Needle 1 K1, M1, knit until the last stitch, M1, k1.
Needle 2 K1, M1, knit until the last stitch, M1, k1.
Then knit a round without increasing.

Repeat these 2 rounds until you have a total of 66 (74) stitches—33 (37) stitches on each needle.

Note: If you prefer a pointier toe, you can cast on fewer stitches, but be sure to increase until you have 33 (37) stitches on each of the 2 needles.

Start the lace pattern:
You will work the chart over needle 1 only (the instep stitches) and will knit across needle 2.
Row 1 On needle 1, k0 (2), work row 1 of the lace chart over the next 33 stitches, k0 (2). Knit across the stitches on needle 2.
Row 2 (and all even-numbered rows) Knit across the stitches on needle 1 and needle 2.
Continue in this manner, working

as many repeats of the 32-row chart as necessary until approximately 3" (7.5cm) shy of the total length of the foot.

CREATE THE GUSSET
Round 1 Work across needle 1 in the lace pattern. Needle 2 (sole stitches): K1, M1, knit across to the last stitch, M1, k1.
Round 2 Work across needle 1 in the lace pattern. Needle 2 (sole stitches): Knit all stitches.
Repeat rounds 1 and 2 until you have 55 (61) stitches total on needle 2.
Work in pattern across the stitches on needle 1.

TURN THE HEEL
You will now work back and forth on the stitches on needle 2 and

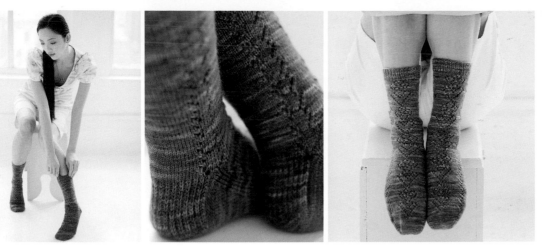

will not knit the stitches on needle 1 while turning the heel. Turn the heel as follows:

Row 1 (RS) K37 (41), kf&b, k1, w&t.

Row 2 P22 (24), pf&b, p1, w&t.

Row 3 K20 (22), kf&b, k1, w&t.

Row 4 P18 (20), pf&b, p1, w&t.

Row 5 K16 (18), kf&b, k1, w&t.

Row 6 P14 (16), pf&b, p1, w&t.

Row 7 K12 (14), kf&b, k1, w&t.

Row 8 P10 (12), pf&b, p1, w&t.

Needle 2 now holds 63 (69) stitches, having just completed a wrong-side row. On the right side, knit to the end of needle 2, knitting each wrap together with the stitch it wraps. Work across the instep stitches on needle 1 in the lace pattern.

HEEL FLAP

Work back and forth on the heel stitches:

Row 1 (RS) K47 (52) (knitting each wrap together with the stitch it wraps), ssk, turn.

Row 2 Sl1, p31 (35), p2tog, turn.

Row 3 *Sl1, k1; repeat from * 16 (18) times, ssk, turn.

Repeat rows 2 and 3 until all of the side stitches have been worked, and end having worked row 2. Needle 2 now holds 33 (37) stitches.

Begin working in the round again. You will continue to work the lace chart on needle 1. On needle 2, work as follows, ensuring that you are on the same row as worked on needle 1: K0 (2), work the first 5 stitches of the lace chart, k23, work the last 5 stitches of the lace chart, k0 (2).

FINISHING

When your sock is 1" (2.5cm) short of the desired leg length, work in k1, p1 ribbing for 1" (2.5cm). Bind off very loosely in rib.

SHERI'S POSIES SOCKS

key

☐	K
/	K2TOG
\	SSK
λ	SL 1 K2TOG, PSSO
O	YO

lace chart

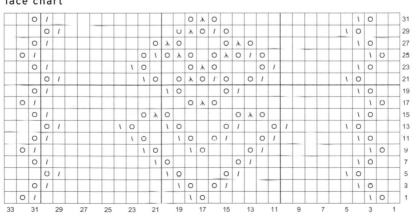

TEXTURED GANSEY SOCKS

ONE OF MY FIRST LOVES IN KNITTING WAS THE BRITISH FISHER gansey. Ganseys are fishermen's pullover sweaters that were popular in the nineteenth and early twentieth centuries. Each fishing village would have its own pattern, and each knitter might knit variations of her village's pattern to make her own sweaters completely unique. Most gansey patterns consisted simply of knit and purl stitch combinations, though some incorporated cables and a bit of lace as well.

I love that the combination of simple knits and purls can make such a striking garment. So, of course, I had to include some socks inspired by ganseys. One great thing about gansey socks is that they are easy to knit. If you can knit and purl, you can make the socks in this section. You will achieve the best results by using solid-color yarns for these designs so that the texture is shown to its best advantage.

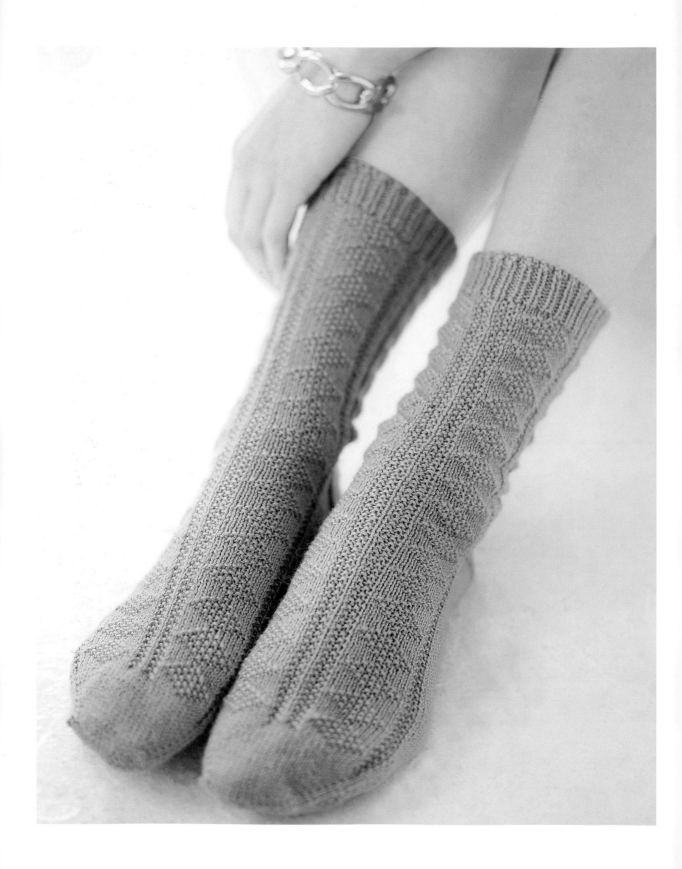

DIAMOND GANSEY SOCKS

DIAMOND GANSEY SOCKS (CONTINUED)

THESE SOCKS WITH SEED STITCH BORDERS AND CLASSIC GANSEY DIAMONDS ARE EASY TO KNIT AND LOVELY TO BEHOLD. KNIT THESE SOCKS IN A LIGHT RATHER THAN VIVID SHADE TO MAKE THE PATTERNING STAND OUT. IF YOU KNIT THEM IN A "GUY" COLOR, THEY MAKE GREAT MEN'S SOCKS.

SIZE: M (L), 8¼ (9¼)" (21 [23.5]cm)

GAUGE: 8 stitches and 12 rows = 1" (2.5cm) in stockinette stitch

NEEDLES: 2 US size 0 (2mm) circular needles (or 1 long circular needle), or size needed to obtain gauge

YARN USED: 2 skeins Louet Gems Fingering, 100% merino wool, 1¾ oz (50g), 185 yd (169m), Aqua (1) Superfine

TOE
Using a Turkish Cast-On, Figure-Eight Cast-On, or Judy's Magic Cast-On (page 20), cast on a total of 30 (34) stitches—15 (17) stitches on each needle. Knit across the stitches on each needle once. On the next round, increase 4 stitches as follows:

Needle 1 K1, M1, knit until the last stitch, M1, k1.

Needle 2 K1, M1, knit until the last stitch, M1, k1.

Then knit a round without increasing.

Repeat these 2 rounds until you have a total of 66 (74) stitches—33 (37) stitches on each needle.

Note: If you prefer a pointier toe, you can cast on fewer stitches, but be sure to increase until you have 33 (37) stitches on each of the 2 needles.

Start the pattern:
You will work the chart over needle 1 only (the instep stitches) and will knit across needle 2.

Row 1 On Needle 1, work row 1 of the chart over the next 33 (37) stitches. Needle 2: Knit across all stitches.

Continue in this manner, working as many repeats of the 10-row chart as necessary until approximately 3" (7.5cm) shy of the total length of the foot.

CREATE THE GUSSET
Round 1 Work across needle 1 in pattern. Needle 2 (sole stitches): K1, M1, knit across to the last stitch, M1, k1.

Round 2 Work across needle 1 in pattern. Needle 2 (sole stitches): Knit all stitches.

Repeat rounds 1 and 2 until you have 55 (61) stitches total on needle 2.

Work in pattern across the stitches on needle 1.

TURN THE HEEL
You will now work back and forth on the stitches on needle 2 and will not knit the stitches on needle 1 while turning the heel. Turn the heel as follows:

Row 1 (RS) K37 (41), kf&b, k1, w&t.

Row 2 P22 (24), pf&b, p1, w&t.

Row 3 K20 (22), kf&b, k1, w&t.

Row 4 P18 (20), pf&b, p1, w&t.

Row 5 K16 (18), kf&b, k1, w&t.

Row 6 P14 (16), pf&b, p1, w&t.

Row 7 K12 (14), kf&b, k1, w&t.

Row 8 P10 (12), pf&b, p1, w&t. Needle 2 now holds 63 (69) stitches, having just completed a wrong-side row. On the right side, knit to the end of needle 2, knitting each wrap together with the stitch it wraps. Work across the instep stitches on needle 1 in pattern.

HEEL FLAP

Work back and forth on the heel stitches:

Row 1 (RS) K47 (52) (knitting each wrap together with the stitch it wraps), ssk, turn.
Row 2 Sl1, p31 (35), p2tog, turn.
Row 3 *Sl1, k1; repeat from * 16 (18) times, ssk, turn.
Repeat rows 2 and 3 until all of the side stitches have been worked, and end having worked row 2. Needle 2 now holds 33 (37) stitches.
Begin working in the round again. Making sure that you are starting in the correct place on the chart, so that it corresponds with the chart on needle 1, work across needle 2 in the same manner as described for needle 1.

FINISHING

When your sock is 1" (2.5cm) short of the desired leg length, work in k1, p1 ribbing for 1" (2.5cm). Bind off very loosely in rib.

DIAMOND GANSEY SOCKS

key
☐ K
• P

large lace chart

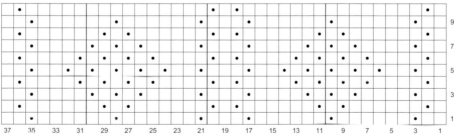

37 35 33 31 29 27 25 23 21 19 17 15 13 11 9 7 5 3 1

medium chart

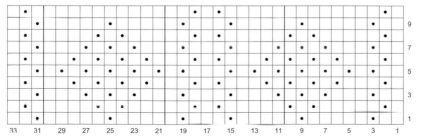

33 31 29 27 25 23 21 19 17 15 13 11 9 7 5 3 1

I HEART TOE-UP SOCKS

I HEART TOE-UP SOCKS (CONTINUED)

ANOTHER TRADITIONAL GANSEY MOTIF IS THE HEART. THIS PATTERN FEATURES A PURLED HEART ON A BACKGROUND OF STOCKINETTE STITCH. THESE SOCKS MAKE A GREAT VALENTINE'S DAY GIFT FOR SOMEONE SPECIAL.

SIZE: M (L), 8¼ (9¼)" (21 [23.5]cm)

GAUGE: 8 stitches and 12 rows = 1" (2.5cm) in stockinette stitch

NEEDLES: 2 US size 0 (2mm) circular needles (or 1 long circular needle), or size needed to obtain gauge

YARN USED: 1 skein J Knits Superwash Me Sock, 75% superwash wool and 25% nylon, 4 oz (113.5g), 420 yd (384m), Oklahoma ⬛ Superfine

---

TOE
Using a Turkish Cast-On, Figure-Eight Cast-On, or Judy's Magic Cast-On (page 20), cast on a total of 30 (34) stitches—15 (17) stitches on each needle. Knit across the stitches on each needle once. On the next round, increase 4 stitches as follows:

Needle 1 K1, M1, knit until the last stitch, M1, k1.

Needle 2 K1, M1, knit until the last stitch, M1, k1.

Then knit a round without increasing.

Repeat these 2 rounds until you have a total of 66 (74) stitches—33 (37) stitches on each needle.

Note: If you prefer a pointier toe, you can cast on fewer stitches, but be sure to increase until you have 33 (37) stitches on each of the 2 needles.

Start the pattern:
You will work the chart over needle 1 only (the instep stitches) and will knit across needle 2.

Size M:
Row 1 On needle 1, work the 33 stitches of row 1 of the chart. Needle 2: Knit across all 33 stitches.

Row 2 On needle 1, work the 33 stitches of row 2 of the chart. Needle 2: Knit across all 33 stitches.

Size L:
Row 1 On needle 1, k1, p1, work the 33 stitches of row 1 of the chart, p1, k1. Needle 2: Knit across all 37 stitches.

Row 2 On needle 1, k1, p1, work the 33 stitches of row 2 of the chart, p1, k1. Needle 2: Knit across all 37 stitches.

For both sizes:
Continue in this manner, working as many repeats of the 12-row chart as necessary until approximately 3" (7.5cm) shy of the total length of the foot.

CREATE THE GUSSET
Round 1 Work across needle 1 in the chart pattern. Needle 2 (sole stitches): K1, M1, knit across to the last stitch, M1, k1.

Round 2 Work across needle 1 in the chart pattern. Needle 2 (sole stitches): Knit all stitches.

Repeat rounds 1 and 2 until you have 55 (61) stitches total on needle 2.

Work in pattern across the stitches on needle 1.

TURN THE HEEL

You will now work back and forth on the stitches on needle 2 and will not work the stitches on needle 1 while turning the heel. Turn the heel as follows:

Row 1 (RS) K37 (41), kf&b, k1, w&t.
Row 2 P22 (24), pf&b, p1, w&t.
Row 3 K20 (22), kf&b, k1, w&t.
Row 4 P18 (20), pf&b, p1, w&t.
Row 5 K16 (18), kf&b, k1, w&t.
Row 6 P14 (16), pf&b, p1, w&t.
Row 7 K12 (14), kf&b, k1, w&t.

Row 8 P10 (12), pf&b, p1, w&t. Needle 2 now holds 63 (69) stitches, having just completed a wrong-side row. On the right side, knit to the end of needle 2, knitting each wrap together with the stitch it wraps. Work across the instep stitches on needle 1 in the chart pattern.

Heel Flap

Work back and forth on the heel stitches on needle 2:

Row 1 (RS) K47 (52) (knitting each wrap together with the stitch it wraps), ssk, turn.
Row 2 Sl1, p31 (35), p2tog, turn.
Row 3 [Sl1, k1] 16 (18) times, ssk, turn.

Repeat rows 2 and 3 until all of the side stitches have been worked, and end having worked row 2. Needle 2 now holds 33 (37) stitches.

Begin working in the round again. If you are in the middle of a heart in the chart, work the stitches on needle 2 as for the foot of the sock until you have gotten to the point where you can start a heart on the back of the sock.

Continue in this manner, working the chart until the leg of the sock is 1" (2.5cm) shy of the desired length.

FINISHING

Work 1" (2.5cm) in k1, p1 ribbing. Bind off loosely in rib.

I HEART TOE-UP SOCKS

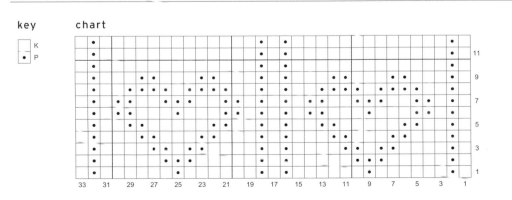

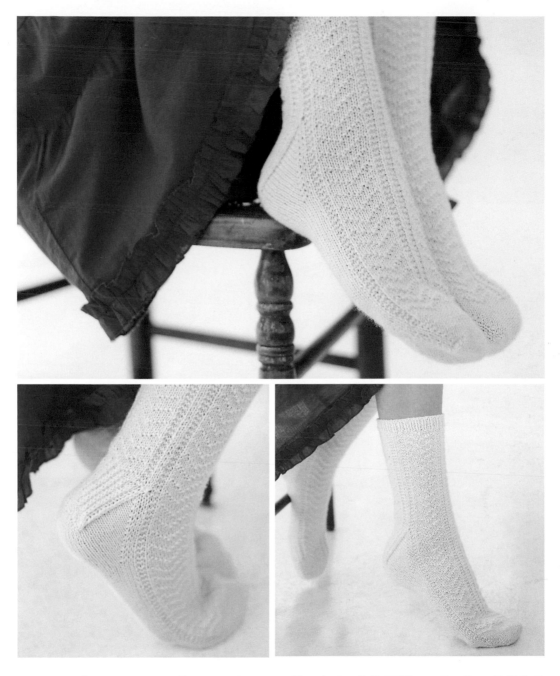

TRADITIONAL GANSEY SOCKS

TRADITIONAL GANSEY SOCKS (CONTINUED)

ONE OF MY FAVORITE GANSEY MOTIFS IS THE SIMPLE "VEE"—IT COULD BE A WAVE IN THE OCEAN OR A SEAGULL FLYING OVERHEAD. THIS SOCK FEATURES VEES WITHIN SEED STITCH BORDERS. LIKE THE DIAMOND GANSEY SOCKS (PAGE 90), THESE WOULD MAKE GREAT GUY SOCKS.

SIZE: M (L), 8¼ (9¼)" (21 [23.5]cm)

GAUGE: 8 stitches and 12 rows = 1" (2.5cm) in stockinette stitch

NEEDLES: 2 US size 0 (2mm) circular needles (or 1 long circular needle), or size needed to obtain gauge

YARN USED: 2 skeins Shibui Knits Sock, 100% superwash merino wool, 1¾ oz (50g), 191 yd (174.5m), Ivory ❶ Superfine

TOE

Using a Turkish Cast-On, Figure-Eight Cast-On, or Judy's Magic Cast-On (page 20), cast on a total of 30 (34) stitches—15 (17) stitches on each needle. Knit across the stitches on each needle once.

On the next round, increase 4 stitches as follows:

Needle 1 K1, M1, knit until the last stitch, M1, k1.

Needle 2 K1, M1, knit until the last stitch, M1, k1.

Then knit a round without increasing.

Repeat these 2 rounds until you have a total of 66 (74) stitches—33 (37) stitches on each needle.

Note: If you prefer a pointier toe, you can cast on fewer stitches, but be sure to increase until you have 33 (37) stitches on each of the 2 needles.

Start the pattern:

You will work the chart over needle 1 only (the instep stitches) and will knit across needle 2.

Row 1: On needle 1, work row 1 of the chart over the next 33 (37) stitches. Needle 2: Knit across all stitches.

Continue in this manner, working as many repeats of the 10-row chart as necessary until approximately 3" (7.5cm) shy of the total length of the foot.

CREATE THE GUSSET

Round 1 Work across needle 1 in pattern. Needle 2 (sole stitches): K1, M1, knit across to the last stitch, M1, k1.

Round 2 Work across needle 1 in pattern. Needle 2 (sole stitches): Knit all stitches.

Repeat rounds 1 and 2 until you have 55 (61) stitches total on needle 2.

Work in pattern across the stitches on needle 1.

TURN THE HEEL

You will now work back and forth on the stitches on needle 2 and will not knit the stitches on needle 1 while turning the heel. Turn the heel as follows:

Row 1 (RS) K37 (41), kf&b, k1, w&t.

Row 2 P22 (24), pf&b, p1, w&t.

Row 3 K20 (22), kf&b, k1, w&t.

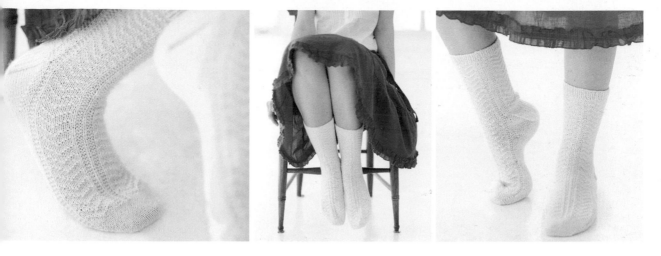

Row 4 P18 (20), pf&b, p1, w&t.
Row 5 K16 (18), kf&b, k1, w&t.
Row 6 P14 (16), pf&b, p1, w&t.
Row 7 K12 (14), kf&b, k1, w&t.
Row 8 P10 (12), pf&b, p1, w&t.
Needle 2 now holds 63 (69) stitches, having just completed a wrong-side row. On the right side, knit to the end of needle 2, knitting each wrap together with the stitch it wraps. Work across the instep stitches on needle 1 in pattern.

HEEL FLAP
Work back and forth on the heel stitches:
Row 1 (RS) K47 (52) (knitting each wrap together with the stitch it wraps), ssk, turn.
Row 2 Sl1, p31 (35), p2tog, turn.
Row 3 [Sl1, k1] 16 (18) times, ssk, turn.
Repeat rows 2 and 3 until all of the side stitches have been worked, and end having worked row 2. Needle 2 now holds 33 (37) stitches.

Begin working in the round again. Making sure that you are starting in the correct place on the chart so that it corresponds with the chart on needle 1, work across needle 2 in the same manner as described for needle 1.

FINISHING
When your sock is 1" (2.5cm) short of the desired leg length, work in k1, p1 ribbing for 1" (2.5cm). Bind off very loosely in rib.

TRADITIONAL GANSEY SOCKS

key

☐	K
•	P

large chart

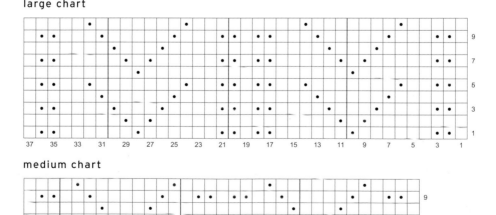

medium chart

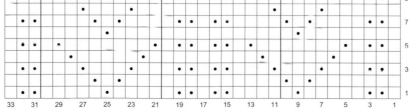

CABLED SOCKS

ANOTHER OF MY KNITTING LOVES IS CABLES. BUT I AM ALWAYS A bit leery of cabled socks, knowing the bulk that cables can add to a garment. I've gotten around the issue of too much bulk with these two patterns. While they are not "true" cabled socks, they use traveling stitches to give the appearance of cables without the bulk.

MOCK CABLE SOCKS

MOCK CABLE SOCKS (CONTINUED)

WHEN YOU KNIT THESE SOCKS, YOU ARE JUST MOVING ONE STITCH AT A TIME RATHER THAN DOING A "REAL" CABLE CROSSING. BUT THE OVERALL EFFECT AMOUNTS TO A DIAGONAL CABLE ON THIS SOCK. MADE IN A MANLY COLOR, THIS IS A GREAT PATTERN FOR CONSERVATIVE GUY SOCKS.

SIZE: M (L), 8 (9)" (20.5 [23]cm)

GAUGE: 7½ stitches and 12 rows = 1" (2.5cm) in stockinette stitch

NEEDLES: 2 US size 0 (2mm) circular needles (or 1 long circular needle), or size needed to obtain gauge

YARN USED: 1 skein Cherry Tree Hill Supersock Solids, 100% luxury merino fingering weight, 4 oz (113.5g), 420 yd (384m), Slate (**1**) Superfine

---

TOE
Using a Turkish Cast-On, Figure-Eight Cast-On, or Judy's Magic Cast-On (page 20), cast on a total of 30 (34) stitches—15 (17) stitches on each needle. Knit across the stitches on each needle once.
On the next round, increase 4 stitches as follows:
Needle 1 K1, M1, knit until the last stitch, M1, k1.
Needle 2 K1, M1, knit until the last stitch, M1, k1.
Then knit a round without increasing.
Repeat these 2 rounds until you have a total of 66 (74) stitches—33 (37) stitches on each needle.

Note: If you prefer a pointier toe, you can cast on fewer stitches,

but be sure to increase until you have 33 (37) stitches on each of the 2 needles.

Start the pattern:
You will work the chart over needle 1 only (the instep stitches) and will knit across needle 2. Continue in this manner, working as many repeats of the 4-row chart as necessary until approximately 3" (7.5cm) shy of the total length of the foot.

CREATE THE GUSSET
Round 1 Work across needle 1 in the chart pattern. Needle 2 (sole stitches): K1, M1, knit across to the last stitch, M1, k1.
Round 2 Work across needle 1 in the chart pattern. Needle 2 (sole stitches): Knit all stitches.

Repeat rounds 1 and 2 until you have 55 (61) stitches total on needle 2.
Work in pattern across the stitches on needle 1.

TURN THE HEEL
You will now work back and forth on the stitches on needle 2 and will not knit the stitches on needle 1 while turning the heel. Turn the heel as follows:
Row 1 (RS) K37 (41), kf&b, k1, w&t.
Row 2 P22 (24), pf&b, p1, w&t.
Row 3 K20 (22), kf&b, k1, w&t.
Row 4 P18 (20), pf&b, p1, w&t.
Row 5 K16 (18), kf&b, k1, w&t.
Row 6 P14 (16), pf&b, p1, w&t.
Row 7 K12 (14), kf&b, k1, w&t.
Row 8 P10 (12), pf&b, p1, w&t.
Needle 2 now holds 63 (69) stitches, having just completed a

wrong-side row. On the right side, knit to the end of needle 2, knitting each wrap together with the stitch it wraps. Work across the instep stitches on needle 1 in the lace pattern.

HEEL FLAP

Work back and forth on the heel stitches:

Row 1 (RS) K47 (52) (knitting each wrap together with the stitch it wraps), ssk, turn.

Row 2 Sl1, p31 (35), p2tog, turn.

Row 3 [Sl1, k1] 16 (18) times, ssk, turn.

Repeat rows 2 and 3 until all of the side stitches have been worked, and end having worked row 2. Needle 2 now holds 33 (37) stitches.

Begin working in the round again. You will continue to work the chart on needle 1. Begin working the chart over needle 2, ensuring that you are starting in the correct place on the chart so that it corresponds with the chart on needle 1.

FINISHING

When your sock is the desired leg length, bind off very loosely in the cable pattern.

MOCK CABLE SOCKS

key

	K
	P
	Place next stitch on cable needle and hold at back of work. K1, then K1 from cable needle
	Place next stitch on cable needle and hold at front of work. K1, then K1 from cable needle

large chart

37 35 33 31 29 27 25 23 21 19 17 15 13 11 9 7 5 3 1

medium chart

33 31 29 27 25 23 21 19 17 15 13 11 9 7 5 3 1

BAVARIAN CABLE SOCKS

BAVARIAN CABLE SOCKS (CONTINUED)

THIS SOCK, TOO, DOES NOT HAVE A TRUE CABLE. RATHER, IT HAS A BAVARIAN TRAVELING STITCH THAT CREATES A PRETTY LATTICE ON THE SOCKS. YOU WILL WANT TO USE A SOLID-COLOR YARN FOR THESE SOCKS SO THAT THE TRAVELING STITCHES "POP." IT'S A GOOD IDEA, TOO, TO USE A YARN THAT ISN'T TOO SPLITTY BECAUSE THERE IS A LOT OF STITCH MANIPULATION GOING ON IN THE PATTERN.

SIZE: M (L), 8 (9)" (20.5 [23]cm)

GAUGE: 7½ stitches and 12 rows = 1" (2.5cm) in stockinette stitch

NEEDLES: 2 US size 0 (2mm) circular needles (or 1 long circular needle), or size needed to obtain gauge

YARN USED: 2 skeins Louet Gems Fingering, 100% merino wool, 1¾ oz (50g), 185 yd (169m), Ginger 🔟 Superfine

---

TOE

Using a Turkish Cast-On, Figure-Eight Cast-On, or Judy's Magic Cast-On (page 20), cast on a total of 30 (34) stitches—15 (17) stitches on each needle. Knit across the stitches on each needle once. On the next round, increase 4 stitches as follows:

Needle 1 K1, M1, knit until the last stitch, M1, k1.

Needle 2 K1, M1, knit until the last stitch, M1, k1.

Then knit a round without increasing.

Repeat these 2 rounds until you have a total of 66 (74) stitches—33 (37) stitches on each needle.

Note: If you prefer a pointier toe, you can cast on fewer stitches, but be sure to increase until you have (33, 37) stitches on each of the 2 needles.

Next round Knit, increasing 4 (3) stitches evenly over needle 1 so that you now have 37 (40) stitches on needle 1. Knit across the 33 (37) stitches on needle 2.

Start the pattern:

You will work the chart over needle 1 only (the instep stitches) and will knit across the stitches on needle 2.

Note: If you are a particularly tight knitter, you might want to go up a needle size for needle 1 so that you are not working the twists and cables too tightly.

Size M:

Row 1 On needle 1, work all of the stitches of the first row of the chart once; then knit stitches 2–10 of the chart 3 times. Needle 2: Knit across the stitches.

Row 2 On needle 1, work all of the stitches of the second row of the chart once; then knit stitches 2–10 of the chart 3 times. Needle 2: Knit across the stitches.

Size L:

Row 1 On needle 1, work the first row of the chart 4 times. Needle 2: Knit across the stitches.

Row 2 On needle 1, work the second row of the chart 4 times. Needle 2: Knit across the stitches.

For both sizes:

Continue in this manner, working as many repeats of the chart as necessary until approximately 3" (7.5cm) shy of the total length of the foot.

CREATE THE GUSSET

Round 1 Work across needle 1 in the pattern. Needle 2 (sole stitches): K1, M1, knit across to the last stitch, M1, k1.

Round 2 Work across needle 1 in the pattern. Needle 2 (sole stitches): Knit all stitches.

Repeat rounds 1 and 2 until you have 55 (61) stitches total on needle 2.

Work in pattern across the stitches on needle 1.

TURN THE HEEL

You will now work back and forth on the stitches on needle 2 and will not work the stitches on needle 1 while turning the heel. Turn the heel as follows:

Row 1 (RS) K37 (41), kf&b, k1, w&t.
Row 2 P22 (24), pf&b, p1, w&t.
Row 3 K20 (22), kf&b, k1, w&t.
Row 4 P18 (20), pf&b, p1, w&t.
Row 5 K16 (18), kf&b, k1, w&t.
Row 6 P14 (16), pf&b, p1, w&t.
Row 7 K12 (14), kf&b, k1, w&t.
Row 8 P10 (12), pf&b, p1, w&t.

Needle 2 now holds 63 (69) stitches, having just completed a wrong-side row. On the right side, knit to the end of needle 2, knitting each wrap together with the stitch it wraps. Work across the instep stitches on needle 1 in pattern.

HEEL FLAP

Work back and forth on the heel stitches on needle 2:
Row 1 (RS) K47 (52) (knitting each wrap together with the stitch it wraps), ssk, turn.
Row 2 Sl1, p31 (35), p2tog, turn.
Row 3 *Sl1, k1; repeat from * 16 (18) times, ssk, turn.

Repeat rows 2 and 3 until all of the side stitches have been worked, and end having worked row 2. Needle 2 now holds 33 (37) stitches.

Begin working in the round again as follows:

Next round: Work across needle 1 in the chart pattern. On needle 2, knit, increasing 4 (3) stitches evenly over needle 2 so that you now have 37 (40) stitches on needle 2.

Start the pattern. Making sure that you are starting in the correct place on the chart, so that it corresponds with the chart on needle 1, work across needle 2 in the same manner as described for needle 1.

FINISHING

When you are 1" (2.5cm) short of the desired length of the sock, work 1" (2.5cm) of twisted ribbing: k1, tbl, p1, repeat around. Bind off loosely in rib.

BAVARIAN CABLE SOCKS

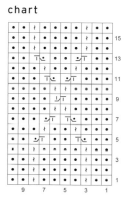

chart

key

† K through back loop
• P

T SL next st to cable needle, hold at front of work, P the next st, then K through back loop the stitch on the cable needle
T SL next st to cable needle, hold at back of work, K through back loop the next st, then P the stitch on the cable needle
T SL next st to cable needle, hold at back of work, K through back loop the next st, then K through back loop the stitch on the cable needle

SPORTWEIGHT SOCKS

ARE YOU AN IMPATIENT KNITTER? PERHAPS YOU NEED A GIFT FOR

someone special in a hurry. Or maybe you want to make yourself some

extra-thick and cozy winter socks. Here are three patterns for sport-

weight yarn that work up in a snap. They all feature the gusset heel,

which is not as bulky as the slip stitch heel.

VAN DYKE SOCKS

VAN DYKE SOCKS (CONTINUED)

A SIMPLE, CLASSIC VAN DYKE LACE PATTERN CLIMBS UP THESE SOCKS. THE PATTERN IS WRITTEN FOR FOUR SIZES, SO YOU CAN MAKE A PAIR FOR EVERYONE.

SIZE: S (M, L, XL), 7½ (8, 8½, 9)" (19 [20.5, 21.5, 23]cm)

GAUGE: 6½ stitches and 9 rows = 1" (2.5cm) in stockinette stitch

NEEDLES: 1 set US size 2 (2.75mm) double-pointed needles, or size needed to obtain gauge

YARN USED: 1 skein Dream in Color Classy, 100% superfine Australian superwash merino wool, 4 oz (113.5g), 250 yd (228.5m), Happy Forest 🇺🇸 Fine

---

Note: The pattern repeat for this chart is 10 rows. Note that only odd-numbered rows are shown on the chart; even-numbered rows are all plain knit.

TOE

Using 2 needles and a Turkish Cast-On, Figure-Eight Cast-On, or Judy's Magic Cast-On (page 20), cast on a total of 24 stitches—12 on each needle. Work the stitches as described in your cast-on method and divide them over your double-pointed needles so that there are 6 stitches on each of 4 needles. Knit one round even. On the next round, increase 4 stitches as follows:

Needle 1 K1, M1, knit to the end of the needle.

Needle 2 Knit until the last stitch, M1, k1.

Needle 3 K1, M1, knit to the end of the needle.

Needle 4 Knit until the last stitch, M1, k1.

Then knit around without increasing.

Repeat these 2 rounds until you have a total of 48 (52, 56, 60) stitches, separated as follows:

Needle 1 (instep) 12 (13, 14, 15) stitches

Needle 2 (instep) 12 (13, 14, 15) stitches

Needle 3 (sole) 12 (13, 14, 15) stitches

Needle 4 (sole) 12 (13, 14, 15) stitches

Start the lace pattern:

Needle 1 K0 (1, 2, 3), work the lace chart over the next 11 stitches, k1.

Needle 2 K1, work the lace chart over the next 11 stitches, k0 (1, 2, 3).

Needles 3 and 4 Knit across.

Work the foot until you reach the point where your foot connects to the ankle, or approximately 2 to 2½" (5cm–6.5cm) shy of the total length of the foot.

CREATE THE GUSSET

Round 1 Work across needle 1 and needle 2 (the instep stitches) in the chart pattern. Needle 3 (sole stitches): K1, M1, knit across the remaining stitches. Needle 4: Knit until the last stitch, M1, k1.

Round 2 Work across needle 1 and needle 2 (the instep stitches) in the chart pattern. Needle 3 and Needle 4: Knit all stitches.

Repeat rounds 1 and 2 until you

have 40 (44, 48, 52) stitches total on needles 3 and 4.
Work in pattern across the stitches on needles 1 and 2.

TURN THE HEEL

Slip all stitches from needles 3 and 4 onto 1 needle. You will work back and forth on these stitches and will not knit the stitches on needles 1 and 2 while turning the heel. Turn the heel as follows:
Row 1 K23 (25, 27, 29), ssk, k1, turn.

Row 2 Sl1, p7, p2tog, p1, turn.
Row 3 Sl1, k8, ssk, k1, turn.
Row 4 Sl1, p9, p2tog, p1, turn.
Row 5 Sl1, k10, ssk, k1, turn.
Row 6 Sl1, p11, p2tog, p1, turn.
Continue in this manner until all of the stitches are worked and you have 24 (26, 28, 30) stitches on the needle. Divide these 24 (26, 28, 30) stitches over 2 needles and begin working in the round again. You now have 12 (13, 14, 15) stitches each on needles 3 and 4. Work the chart pattern

over needles 3 and 4, setting it up as you did for needles 1 and 2, ensuring that you are starting in the correct place on the chart so that it corresponds with the chart on needles 1 and 2.
Work in pattern until your sock is 1" (2.5cm) short of the desired leg length.

FINISHING

Work in k2, p2 ribbing for 1" (2.5cm). Bind off very loosely in rib.

VAN DYKE SOCKS

---

key

	K
/	K2TOG
\	SSK
o	YO

lace chart

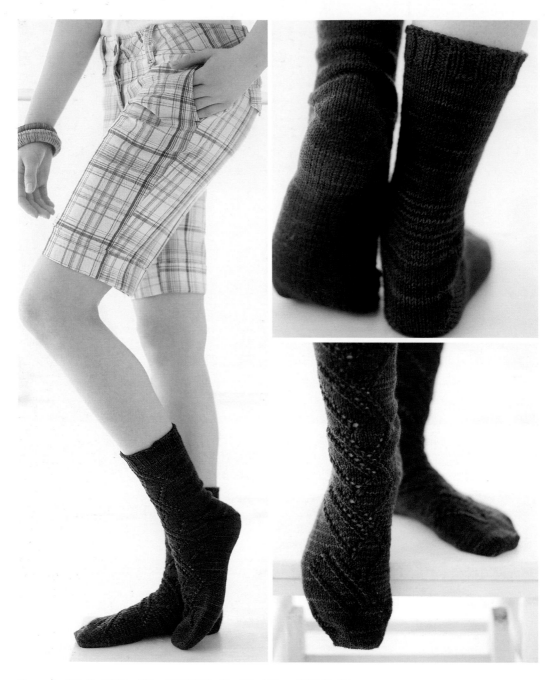

LABYRINTH SOCKS

DON'T GET LOST IN THE LABYRINTH—USE A ROW COUNTER! THESE SOCKS FEATURE A LACE MAZE, AND THE PATTERN IS WRITTEN FOR THREE SIZES. ALTHOUGH THE SAMPLE SOCKS ARE KNIT IN AN ALMOST-SOLID COLORWAY, THESE SOCKS WOULD LOOK BEAUTIFUL KNIT IN A HEATHERED OR SLIGHTLY VARIEGATED YARN.

SIZE: S (M, L), 7½ (8, 8½)" (19 [20.5, 21.5]cm)

GAUGE: 6½ stitches and 9 rows = 1" (2.5cm) in stockinette stitch

NEEDLES: 2 US size 2 (2.75mm) circular needles (or 1 long circular needle), or size needed to obtain gauge

YARN USED: 3 skeins Claudia Hand Painted Yarns Sport Shorts, 100% merino wool, 1¾ oz (50g), 112 yd (102.5m), Ink (2) Fine

---

Note: The pattern repeat for this chart is 26 rows. Note that only odd-numbered rows are shown on the chart; even-numbered rows are all plain knit.

TOE

Using a Turkish Cast-On, Figure-Eight Cast-On, or Judy's Magic Cast-On (page 20), cast on a total of 24 stitches—12 stitches on each needle. Work the stitches as described in your cast-on method, and knit 1 round even. On the next round, increase 4 stitches as follows:

Needle 1 K1, M1, knit until the last stitch, M1, k1.

Needle 2 K1, M1, knit until the last stitch, M1, k1.

Then knit a round without increasing.

Repeat these 2 rounds until you have a total of 48 (52, 56) stitches.

Separate the stitches as follows:

Needle 1 (instep) 24 (26, 28) stitches

Needle 2 (sole) 24 (26, 28) stitches

Start the lace pattern:

Needle 1 K1 (2, 3), work the lace chart over the next 22 stitches, k1 (2, 3).

Needle 2 Knit across.

Work the foot until you reach the point where your foot connects to the ankle, or approximately 2 to 2½" (5cm–6.5cm) shy of the total length of the foot.

CREATE THE GUSSET

Round 1 Work across needle 1 (the instep stitches) in the lace pattern. Needle 2 (sole stitches): K1, M1, knit across to the last stitch, M1, k1.

Round 2 Work across needle 1 (the instep stitches) in the lace pattern. Needle 2: Knit all stitches.

Repeat rounds 1 and 2 until you have 40 (44, 48) stitches on needle 2.

Work in pattern across the stitches on needle 1.

LABYRINTH SOCKS (CONTINUED)

TURN THE HEEL

You will work back and forth on the stitches on needle 2 and will not work the stitches on needle 1 while turning the heel. On needle 2, turn the heel as follows:

Row 1 K23 (25, 27), ssk, k1, turn.
Row 2 Sl1, p7, p2tog, p1, turn.
Row 3 Sl1, k8, ssk, k1, turn.
Row 4 Sl1, p9, p2tog, p1, turn.
Row 5 Sl1, k10, ssk, k1, turn.
Row 6 Sl1, p11, p2tog, p1, turn.

Continue in this manner until all of the stitches are worked and you have 24 (26, 28) stitches on the needle. Resume working in the round, working the lace chart as set over needle 1, and knitting all stitches on needle 2.

Work in pattern until your sock is 1" (2.5cm) short of the desired leg length.

FINISHING

Work in k2, p2 ribbing for 1" (2.5cm). Bind off very loosely in rib.

LABYRINTH SOCKS

key

(blank)	K
/	K2TOG
\	SSK
o	YO

lace chart

			\	o		\	o			o	/						o	/				25
		\	o	\	o		\	o								o	/					23
	\	o			\	o		\	o					o	/							21
\	o			\	o		\	o				o	/									19
\	o			\	o		\	o		o	/											17
	\	o			\	o		\	o													15
		\	o		\	o		\	o													13
			\	o		\	o		\	o												11
				\	o		\	o		\	o											9
				\	o		\	o		\	o											7
					\	o		o	/		\	o										5
						\	o	o	/			\	o									3
							\	o					\	o								1
	21		19		17		15		13		11		9		7		5		3		1	

SERPENTINE SOCKS

SERPENTINE SOCKS (CONTINUED)

THESE SNAKES ARE NOT POISONOUS, AND THEY WOULDN'T DREAM OF HURTING YOU. THEY ARE ACTUALLY VERY OBEDIENT AND FALL INTO PLACE NICELY AS YOU KNIT. THE SOCK IS DESIGNED FOR THREE SIZES.

SIZE: S (M, L), 7½ (8, 8½)" (19 [20.5, 21.5]cm)

GAUGE: 6½ stitches and 9 rows = 1" (2.5cm) in stockinette stitch

NEEDLES: 2 US size 2 (2.75mm) circular needles (or 1 long circular needle), or size needed to obtain gauge

YARN USED: 1 skein Fiesta Boomerang, extra fine superwash merino wool, 5 oz (140g), 320 yd (292.5m), Painted Desert (2) Fine

---

Note: The pattern repeat for this chart is 16 rows. Note that only odd-numbered rows are shown on the chart; even-numbered rows are all plain knit.

TOE

Using a Turkish Cast-On, Figure-Eight Cast-On, or Judy's Magic Cast-On (page 20), cast on a total of 24 stitches—12 stitches on each needle. Work the stitches as described in your cast-on method and knit 1 round even. On the next round, increase 4 stitches as follows:

Needle 1 K1, M1, knit until the last stitch, M1, k1.

Needle 2 K1, M1, knit until the last stitch, M1, k1.

Then knit a round without increasing.

Repeat these 2 rounds until you have a total of 48 (52, 56) stitches.

Separate the stitches as follows:

Needle 1 (instep) 24 (26, 28) stitches

Needle 2 (sole) 24 (26, 28) stitches

Start the lace pattern:

Needle 1 K1 (2, 3), work the lace chart over the next 22 stitches, k1 (2, 3).

Needle 2 Knit across.

Work the foot until you reach the point where your foot connects to the ankle, or approximately 2 to 2½"

(5cm to 6.5cm) shy of the total length of the foot.

CREATE THE GUSSET

Round 1 Work across needle 1 (the instep stitches) in the lace pattern. Needle 2 (sole stitches): K1, M1, knit across to the last stitch, M1, k1.

Round 2 Work across needle 1 (the instep stitches) in the lace pattern. Needle 2: Knit all stitches.

Repeat rounds 1 and 2 until you have 44 (48, 52) stitches on needle 2.

Work in pattern across the stitches on needle 1.

TURN THE HEEL

You will work back and forth on the stitches on needle 2 and will not work the stitches on needle 1 while turning the heel. On needle 2, turn the heel as follows:

Row 1 K23 (25, 27), ssk, k1, turn.
Row 2 Sl1, p7, p2tog, p1, turn.
Row 3 Sl1, k8, ssk, k1, turn.
Row 4 Sl1, p9, p2tog, p1, turn.

Row 5 Sl1, k10, ssk, k1, turn.
Row 6 Sl1, p11, p2tog, p1, turn.
Continue in this manner until all of the stitches are worked and you have 24 (26, 28) stitches on the needle. Resume working in the round, working the lace chart as set over needle 1. On needle 2, k1 (2, 3), work the lace chart across the next 22 stitches (making sure you are on the same

row of the chart as for needle 1), k1 (2, 3).
Work in pattern until your sock is 1" (2.5cm) short of the desired leg length.

FINISHING

Work in k2, p2 ribbing for 1" (2.5cm). Bind off very loosely in rib.

SERPENTINE SOCKS

key

	K
•	P
O	YO
\	S3K
/	K2TOG

lace chart

21		19		17		15		13		11		9		7		5		3		1	
•		O			/	•			O			/	•			O			/	•	15
•			O		/		•			O			/	•			O		/	•	13
•	O			/		•	O			/		•	O			/		•		•	11
•						•						•						•			9
•	\			O		•	\			O		•	\			O		•			7
•		\			O	•		\			O	•		\			O	•			5
•			\		O	•			\		O	•			\		O	•			3
•						•						•						•			1

ABBREVIATIONS

k—knit

k2tog—knit two together

kf&b—knit in the front and back of the next stitch

m1—make one

p—purl

p2tog—purl two together

pf&b—purl in the front and back of the next stitch

psso—pass slipped stitch over

RS—right side

sl—slip

ssk—Slip one stitch; then slip the next. Insert the left needle into the front loops of the slipped stitches and knit them together from this position (through the back loops)

tbl—through back loops

w&t—Wrap and turn. Bring yarn to the front of the work between the needles, slip the next stitch onto the right-hand needle, bring the yarn around this stitch to the back of the work, slip the stitch back to the left-hand needle, and turn the work to begin working back in the other direction.

yo—yarnover

DEFINITIONS

Bind off. Finish off live stitches at the end of a knitted piece so that the knitted work does not unravel. To bind off in pattern, knit or purl as directed by the pattern and slip the finished stitches over each other until you have only one stitch left. The final stitch is finished by pulling the tail end of the yarn through the last stitch.

Block. Finish a knitted fabric and even out the stitches by moistening with water or steam and shaping to the final measurements. A sock can be blocked by laying the damp piece flat on a towel and manually shaping it to the proper size, or by slipping the damp sock over a sock blocker of the proper size and allowing it to dry.

Cable. A twisted design within the knitted fabric made by crossing a stitch or group of stitches in front or behind each other.

Cable Needle. A small, double-pointed needle, either straight or curved, used to temporarily hold stitches off the work when creating a cable pattern.

Cast off. See Bind off.

Circular needle. A knitting needle that consists of short, straight, or slightly bent rigid needles attached to a flexible cord. You can knit socks on two circular needles or, using the Magic Loop technique (page 23), on one longer circular needle.

Decrease. To reduce the number of stitches in a row. You can decrease one stitch by working two stitches together in a variety of ways. You can decrease two stitches by working three stitches together in a variety of ways: by slipping 1, knitting 2 together, and passing the slipped stitch over the knit 2 together; by slipping 2 knitwise, knitting 1, and passing the 2 slipped stitches over the knit 1; by knitting 3 together (either normally or through the back loops); or by purling 3 together.

Double-pointed needles. Straight needles with a point at each end that are used for knitting socks and other small circular items. Double-pointed needles are usually sold in sets of five.

Gauge. The number of stitches and rows in a set measured area (usually 4" [10cm] square). Knit a swatch to check your gauge to make sure that your finished project will have the correct measurements.

Grafting. A method used to join two active rows of knitting so that seaming will resemble a row of knitting stitches; also known as Kitchener stitch. Socks knitted from the top down will usually require grafting to close up the toe. Toe-up socks need no grafting.

Increase. Add a stitch or stitches to make the knitted piece wider. Common increases are m1 (make one) and yo (yarn over).

Knitwise. Insert the right needle into the front of a stitch from left to right.

Live stitch. A stitch that is being worked on a needle and has not yet been bound off.

Make one. A technique used for increasing stitches.

Marker. A device used to mark a pattern change. Among other things, you can use a ring (metal, plastic, rubber, and so forth) or a loop made from a strand of yarn as a marker.

Purlwise. Insert the right needle into the front of a stitch from right to left.

Ribbing. A combination of knit and purl stitches that creates a stretchy fabric with vertical ridges. Ribbing is commonly found at the beginning and end of sweaters, hats, mittens, and socks.

Right side. The side of fabric shown on the outside (or "public" side) of a project.

Short rows. A shaping method used to add curves, fullness, and shape to a knitted piece. You can use short rows to create toes and heels for socks.

Slip stitch. To move a stitch from one needle to another without working it. You can slip a stitch knitwise or purlwise.

Stitch holder. A tool used to temporarily hold stitches not being worked to prevent them from unraveling. A piece of waste yarn or a circular needle with

point protectors on the ends can be used as a stitch holder.

Work even. Work in the established pattern without increasing or decreasing stitches. Also known as "working straight."

Wrong side. The side of the fabric shown on the inside (or "private" side) of a project.

Yarn over. To make a new stitch by wrapping yarn over the right needle but not working it—sometimes called "yarn forward." Working a yarn over will create a small hole in the work, so it is used in lace patterns.

RESOURCES

YARNS

All of the projects in this book call for materials that are readily available either at yarn stores near you or online. The following list of suppliers will help you find all the materials you need to complete the projects in the book. If you have trouble finding a product, consult the websites listed to locate a distributor near you.

Blue Moon Fiber Arts:
www.bluemoonfiberarts.com
866-802-9687

Cherry Tree Hill:
www.cherryyarn.com
802-525-3311

Claudia Hand Painted Yarns:
www.claudiaco.com
540-433-1140

Colinette:
www.colinette.com
01938 810128

Dream in Color:
www.dreamincoloryarn.com

Fiesta Yarns:
www.fiestayarns.com
505-892-5008

Fleece Artist:
www.fleeceartist.com
902-462-0800

J Knits:
www.j-knits.com
888-395-8261

Lisa Souza Knitwear and Dyeworks:
www.lisaknit.com
530-647-1183

Lorna's Laces:
www.lornaslaces.net
773-935-3803

Louet:
www.louet.com
613-925-1405

Shibui Knits:
www.shibuiknits.com
971-678-1721

ONLINE HELP

While yarn stores offer classes and are a great resource for beginning knitters, everything I ever learned about knitting socks, I learned online. Although this is a slight exaggeration, it is true that you can learn a lot about sock knitting if you have a computer and an Internet connection. Many wonderful websites offer help and tutorials for all things related to sock knitting.

Persistent Illusion
Detailed instructions for working Judy's Magic Cast-On technique can be found on Judy Becker's website, Persistent Illusion: www.persistentillusion.com.

Socknitters
Cyberclasses, tips and tricks, patterns, links, and an e-mail group can be found on the Socknitters website: www.socknitters.com.

Ravelry

Ravelry is like MySpace for knitters. This site has, among other things, a library of free knitting patterns and many, many special interest groups. There are well over two hundred groups and forums about socks on Ravelry: www.ravelry.com.

KnittingHelp

Knitting Help features many videos demonstrating knitting techniques. If you are a visual learner, this is a great resource: www.knittinghelp.com.

YouTube

YouTube is a treasure trove of video tutorials. Do a search for "knit socks," and you'll be rewarded with many great tutorials. You can even search for a specific technique, such as Judy's Magic Cast-On or the Turkish Cast-On: www.youtube.com.

CYCA	1 SUPER FINE	2 FINE	3 LIGHT	4 MEDIUM	5 BULKY
Yarn Weight	Lace, Fingering, Sock	Sport	DK, Light Worsted	Worsted, Aran	Chunky
Avg. Knitted Gauge over 4" (10cm)	27-32 sts	23-26 sts	21-24 sts	16-20 sts	12-15 sts
Recommended Needle in US Size Range	1-3	3-5	5-7	7-9	9-11
Recommended Needle in Metric Size Range	2.25-3.25mm	3.25-3.75mm	3.75-4.5mm	4.5-5.5mm	5.5-8mm

ACKNOWLEDGMENTS

This book would not have been possible without the help of a number of generous people.

Thank you to Blue Moon Fiber Arts, the Loopy Ewe, and Lisa Souza Knitwear and Dyeworks for their generosity in donating the yarn for the socks in this book.

A special thank-you to my friend Sheri Berger at the Loopy Ewe for helping me choose colors and yarns for a number of these projects and for listening to me patiently and offering advice and support whenever I phoned her and rambled on and on about all things socks.

Thank you to Judy Becker for giving me permission to document in this book her marvelous technique for starting toe-up socks: Judy's Magic Cast-On.

Thank you to Ian Ories, who patiently and meticulously took the photographs used to create the illustrations of the techniques demonstrated in this book. Thanks also to Ian for wearing and enjoying the socks I knit for him.

Many thanks to my test knitters: Alice Coppa, Sharon Hart, Lindsey-Brooke Hessa, Hariamrit Khalsa, Laura Linneman, Gail Marracci, Daisy Olsen, Jill Smith, and Margaret H. Velard. Not only did these talented women knit the socks in this book beautifully, but they did a great job of troubleshooting the patterns and clarifying the instructions.

Last but most definitely not least, I offer heartfelt thanks to my technical editor, dear friend, and sister-in-socks, Lindsey-Brooke Hessa. L-B scrutinized the patterns closely, asked questions, made suggestions, knit swatches, and, always on the job, telephoned me from restaurants, airports, moving vehicles, and other remote locations with questions and comments. She listened patiently while I ranted and raved, gently guided me back to the proper path when I went off on tangents best not explored, and responded with tact when I made suggestions too ludicrous to repeat here. She never laughed at me. Well, truthfully, she did laugh, but she did it kindly. And at the end of it all, we remain friends. Thanks, L-B!

INDEX

Copyright © 2009 by Wendy D. Johnson

All rights reserved.

Published in the United States by Potter Craft, an imprint of the Crown Publishing Group, a division of Random House, Inc., New York.
www.crownpublishing.com
www.pottercraft.com

POTTER CRAFT and colophon is a registered trademark of Random House, Inc.

Library of Congress Cataloging-in-Publication Data
Johnson, Wendy D.
  Socks from the toe up : essential techniques and patterns from Wendy Knits / Wendy D. Johnson.—1st ed.
      p. cm.
  ISBN 978-0-307-44944-3
  1. Knitting—Patterns. 2. Socks I. Title.
  TT825.J647 2009
  746.43'2041—dc22
                                    2008030250

ISBN: 978-0-307-44944-3
Printed in China

Design by La Tricia Watford
Photography by Alexandra Grablewski
Illustrations by Kara Gott Warner

10 9 8 7 6 5 4 3 2 1

First Edition

The author and publisher would like to thank the Craft Yarn Council of America for providing the yarn weight standards and accompanying icons used in this book. For more information, please visit www.YarnStandards.com.